my soul thirsts

An Invitation to Intimacy with God

Steve Korch

D1025938

Judson Press

Valley Forge

My Soul Thirsts: An Invitation to Intimacy with God

Library of Congress Cataloging-in-Publication Data

Korch, Steve.
     My soul thirsts : an invitation to intimacy with God / Steve Korch.
          p.   cm.
     ISBN 0-8170-1345-8 (pbk. : alk. paper)
     1. Spiritual life.   I. Title.
     BV4501.2.K647   2000
     248.4 – dc21   99-049495

Printed in the U.S.A.
08 07 06 05 04 03 02 01 00
10 9 8 7 6 5 4 3 2

To Ruthie, Jessica, Holly, and Travers,
my most favorite people in the whole world

Contents

Part 3
THE DRAMATIC DISCOVERY

To the Heart's Delight

(searching for trinkets and finding treasure)

in•ti•mate (in′ te mit) [Fr. < L. *intimus*, within] **1.** pertaining to the inmost character of a thing; fundamental; essential **2.** most private or personal **3.** closely acquainted or associated; very familiar **4.** promoting a feeling of privacy, coziness, romance **5.** resulting from careful study or investigation; thorough.

W HAT PICTURE COMES TO YOUR MIND WHEN YOU THINK OF SOME-
one who is genuinely close to God? Is that person young or old? Does that person live in a rustic monastery or an urban condo? How does that person dress? in a leisure suit? in a business suit? maybe in Levi's and a T-shirt? Does that person live a sedentary lifestyle or blitz through a furious schedule each day? Is that person enjoying life? When that person speaks, is it in a cryptic spiritual language or in the current jargon of the day? As you clarify the picture, what makes that person stand out from others? Most importantly, is that person you?

A conversation I had with a young father captures the spiritual experience of so many believers. He spoke appreciatively of growing up in a Christian home. He had attended wonderful churches from as far back as he could remember. Throughout his childhood he had kept his nose clean, even avoiding all of the potential disasters of the adolescent years. He had dated a Christian girl and had kept their relationship pure. He was now a faithful husband and father, a successful salesman, and a church leader. All of this background information set the stage for his wistful conclusion: "Steve, I have done everything right to the best of my ability. I have lived a safe

1

and secure life. But as I sit here today, it seems so bland and incredibly boring. I have never known the excitement of real intimacy with God or the uncertain adventure of living by faith. I feel like I have missed the very heart of what it's all about."

There is a craving inside each of us that longs for something more than any person or possession in this world can offer. It comes from the deepest caverns of the heart. It drives us, frustrates us, and refuses to be ignored. It cannot be satisfied by merely doing what is good or right. It is the core need in everyone's life. It is the need to be in an ever closer relationship with God — spiritual intimacy — like what is expressed in the opening lines of this psalm:

> As the deer pants for the water brooks,
> So my soul longs for You, O God.
> My soul thirsts for God, for the personal God;
> When shall I come near and see the face of God?

> — Psalm 42:1–2 (author's paraphrase)

But, is it possible for real people, living in a real world, to experience intimacy with God? Does the sheer velocity of life make intimacy with God an impossibility? Are the requirements for such a relationship so demanding that only the spiritual elite can achieve them? From a practical standpoint, are you longing for something that is beyond your reach?

Listen, intimacy with God is not only a realistic possibility; it is a promise! It is more than just an intermittent stirring of your heart; it is an essential part of who you are. The very thing you want most in this life is what you were actually designed for. It is what God wants for you. And there is more! In looking for God, you also find yourself — the person you were created to be — doing what you were created to do. While pursuing personal intimacy with God, you will discover personal transformation in yourself.

This project did not begin as a study of intimacy with God. It was launched in a late-night discussion with some good friends, talking about what new life in Christ looks like. In the Bible, the evidence of new life is presented as something that God alone produces in us: a Spirit-generated transformation, an experience that is almost unavoidable, proof of our saving relationship with God. So, we asked ourselves, why is this new life such a struggle for so many believers? Why does it leave so many others feeling disappointed or even bored? As I have sought the answers to these questions, I have found myself repeatedly addressing their vital connection to intimacy with God.

Let me offer an honest confession right at the outset. I didn't write this book because I have all the answers, but as part of my own search for them. I am certain that you and I wrestle with many of the same issues. I admit that while I know much of what it takes to draw close to God, I am not always willing to apply what I know. And yes, there are definitely times when I don't feel close to God and other times when I don't even have a desire to be near. Truthfully, I am just another sojourner, like yourself, traveling through this brief life. But I have learned that apart from God life makes no sense and that the desire for connectedness with the Creator only intensifies with distance.

Now, if my confession doesn't dissuade you, it appears that we will be traveling together for the next twelve chapters. It is my intention to fuel your passion for God and to focus your energies on drawing close to him. I will do my best to clear away the spiritual debris and mark the pathway to intimacy with God. I will attempt to provide a realistic picture of what to expect along the way. The rest is up to you.

Remember, in the core of your being you were created for an intimate relationship with God. Yahweh invites you (even dares you) to seek such a relationship and to pursue it to your heart's delight.

Part 1

The
Ultimate
Possibility

(So this is what it's
like to be close to God!)

─◈ ONE ◈─

Terms of Endearment

(approaching the fire without getting singed)

WHAT HAD HE DONE? TREMBLING WITH A FEAR THAT EXCEEDED anything he had ever experienced before, he fought to gain some sense of reality. The light blazed before him. Why had he come? Was it nothing more than curiosity, or was there something inside him that yearned to come closer? Had he been lured into this?

The day itself was so ordinary. The roughly chiseled landscape around him communicated a harsh disinterest in him. There was very little evidence of life on this obscure mountain in the desolation of Sinai. But the fringes of this impersonal reality around him had blurred now. Here he was, staring down at his own rugged, dusty feet — his leather sandals hastily kicked off, one flopped over the other. The intensity of a presence projected the light of its flames onto his face. Had he come too close? His heart accelerated with the terrifying excitement of the moment.

He had peered into the eyes of the most powerful men on earth, but he was not prepared for the gaze of this yet nameless Ruler. He had commanded armies and subdued entire nations, but he was no match for this. He stood there in his shepherd garb, humbled by his appearance: old, weak, and unimpressive. He had no right to be there. Yet this Awesome One did not send him away but had, in fact, called him by name — "Moses." Not just once. It had been confirmed after a moment's pause — "Moses." He *was* meant to be there. As frightening as it was, the experience contained an emotional rush of adrenaline. It was the edge of intimacy — with God.

In that concentrated moment, while the mortal toes of this man pressed into dust that had been warmed by the heat of holiness, Moses found what everyone who has ever walked this earth craves. Moses was there because he had genuinely sought God. God was there because he desired to be found.

Years later, Moses passionately spoke the language of God's heart to the hearts of God's people:

> If...you seek the LORD your God, you will find him if you look for him with all your heart and with all your soul. (Deuteronomy 4:29, NIV)

Moses wasn't calling upon people to go search for God. They knew where God was, having spent forty years walking in the shadow of his presence. This was something much greater. It was the answer to a heart longing for intimacy with God. These people were being called into a love relationship of such proportions that it would require the entire being of anyone daring to pursue it:

> Love the LORD your God with all your heart and with all your soul and with all your might. (Deuteronomy 6:5)

To love someone to this degree is to worship that person, which is exactly the point. Such love is the very essence of worship. It is becoming completely absorbed in someone else, drawing so close that you step into that person's heart as a trusted friend — and even more, that you actually feel the pulse of that heart.

The Kiss

The two primary words employed in the Scriptures to communicate worship give great insight into the awesome nature of intimacy with God. The Hebrew term in the Old Testament means "to bow down." It conveys the idea of recognizing the infinite distinction between us and God. It physically puts us in our place. Bent over, with our faces to the ground, we acknowledge that God is the Creator and we are the creatures. It is a personal dethroning of our lofty self-images.

The other term is found in the Greek vocabulary of the New Testament. It is a word that literally means "to kiss toward." Therefore, it could be said that to worship God is to kiss toward heaven. Can you picture the imagery captured in this word? It is a tender expression of love directed toward God. It is a seal of affection — personal, reserved for an intimate friend.

While the first term emphasizes the distance, the second stresses the closeness. The first is the appropriate response to the majesty of God; the second is the fitting response to the heart of God. I believe it is the second word for worship, *proskuneō* in the Greek, that captures the essence of intimacy with God.

When Ruthie, the woman to become my wife, and I began dating each other, we decided to elevate the physical expressions of our relationship by attaching meaning to each of them. There was, perhaps, an element of idealism in this experiment, but we had each dated others and had discovered how easy it was to lose sight of such meanings. Among other things, we determined that a kiss would be a symbol of love for each other and would be reserved for a point when we authentically felt so close that only a kiss could capture its reality.

I can remember the day I first told Ruthie that I loved her. I can also remember the day she first spoke of her love for me (that was not the same day). And I can vividly recall the emotional fireworks of our first kiss. There was nothing casual or trivial about the experience. The kiss came from two hearts that had drawn close to each other. In a similar manner, God actually longs for us to draw close to him and to experience the awesome thrill of kissing toward heaven.

Beneath the Surface

Intimacy is authentic closeness in a personal relationship. It is about what happens between two individuals who genuinely draw near to one another. It includes the sensations of joyful confidence, gracious understanding, relaxed presence, perpetual attraction, and warm affection. With intimacy, there is a heightened sense of respect that removes the stiff formality that stretches the seams between two people who are unsure of each other. It is both moving toward another and likewise allowing that person the freedom to approach. It brings the delightful experience of sharing personal space in the midst of a very private and alienated world.

"The Latin root of our word for *intimacy* is actually the superlative of *intus*, 'within,' " writes author Paul Thigpen. "So the friend who is intimate is literally the one who is 'most within' us, the one we have taken into the deepest chamber of our heart, into the most inward, private, and vulnerable place we have. The fabric of intimacy is thus a reciprocal familiarity, a move beyond acquaintance with the surface to an understanding of the depths." He goes on to mark spiritual intimacy by saying, "We might describe the reality as a kind of *mutual residence of the heart*, in which Jesus invites us to 'abide' in Him as He 'abides' in us, so that He and the Father can make their 'dwelling' in us (John 14:23; 15:4)."[1]

There are at least three basic components to authentic intimacy. They are shared interest in each other, shared information about each other, and shared emotions with each other.

Shared Interest

At the outset, there must be some basic attraction that fuels the search for a secret passageway into the heart of another person, a mutual desire to remove barriers and allow access to one's soul. Intimacy involves the fascination of discovery and the thrill of being discovered.

It is not difficult to understand why we would be fascinated with God. Everything about him boggles the mind and charms the heart. Exploring the person of God is an exciting adventure that never ends. Not only is there a continuous procession of new features to discover about God, but there is also the lingering delight with everything I already know. I find that certain thoughts strike me as brand-new every time I consider them: for example, the fact that an infinite God is giving me undivided and uninterrupted attention at the same time that he is giving that attention to everyone else or the fact that God loves me so completely that there is not a single conceivable circumstance that can ever come between us. These are amazing!

It is not surprising that you and I should be attracted to God. It is, however, a truly amazing thought that God is attracted to us, insignificant creatures in the midst of a vast universe. Yet the Bible tells us that God is intensely interested in every detail of our lives. He longs for us to share in the vast divine knowledge. Jesus was continually asking questions that demonstrated a genuine interest in those around him. He asked,

- What is really important to you?
- What causes you to become fearful or worried?
- How much value do you place upon yourself?
- What is the status of your relationships?
- What are your thoughts about life? about me?

In any relationship, it is a shared interest *in* each other that attracts two people *toward* each other. Such an attraction is a powerful element in developing intimacy with God.

Shared Information

In addition to shared interest *in* each other, there must also be shared information *about* each other. Intimacy involves knowing and being known. Paul Thigpen says, "Deep mutual knowledge...is the practical content of the term *intimacy*."[2] Such mutual knowledge includes a growing awareness of how each other thinks and why certain thoughts are held. It is knowing the quirks of personality, as well as the secret ambitions, fears, and dreams. More than *knowing* all of that as data, intimacy is understanding and appreciating each detail.

God has opened the doors for intimacy by sharing with us a wealth of personal information. God not only tells us about his nature and character but actually brings us inside his heart. God reveals to us his thoughts and emotions and confides in us his intentions and motives. God trusts us with the mysteries behind his actions.

In Psalm 139, David delighted in the fact that God had explored every corner of his life — that God knew him completely. There was nothing hidden before God. There were no secrets. David was free to relate to God without having to evade embarrassing subjects or avoid contact with certain unpleasant aspects of his life:

> Lord, You have searched me and known me....
> You...are intimately acquainted with all my ways.
> —Psalm 139:1,3

For intimacy to exist, two people must possess a mutual knowledge of each other. God has made it possible for us to draw close by making personal information available to anyone who would want to know him. At the same time, God desires for us to acknowledge the truth about ourselves to him.

Shared Emotion

Intimacy is a matter of the heart. Along with shared interest and shared information, it involves each person giving oneself the freedom to feel the passions of the other's heart. The emotional part of intimacy comes from adopting the same concerns as another person. If two people don't feel the same way about something, a sense of distance dulls the relationship.

Shared emotion is vital to spiritual intimacy. While God is definitely interested in what excites us and in the passions that drive our actions, he can only share that emotion when it is in our best interests and when it is unpolluted by sin. As one who genuinely loves us, God cannot be enthusiastic about anything that is destructive to us or that might move us away from him. But when the things that energize us in this life fit with who we are in relation to God and with how God has designed us to live, then we find God excited about what thrills our hearts and desiring to support us.

God longs for our hearts to be synchronized with his. The prophet Azariah spoke to a king of Judah by the name of Asa, "Listen to me," he said, "The LORD is with you when you are with him. If you seek him, he will be found by you" (2 Chronicles 15:2, NIV). Asa found that when the desires of his heart matched those of God's heart, he had success because "the eyes of the LORD range throughout the earth to strengthen those whose hearts are fully committed to him" (2 Chronicles 16:9, NIV).

Intimacy Deficiency Syndrome

No, intimacy deficiency syndrome (IDS) is not officially listed (at the writing of this book) among the ever expanding list of personality disorders that plague our society today.[3] But the most authoritative text on the function and dysfunction of humans, the Bible, describes an intimacy deficiency syndrome that afflicts everyone. The Bible details the cause, the symptoms, and the treatment for IDS.

Design Flaw?

We all have a need for relating to other people on an intimate level. In Genesis 2:18, God said that it was not good for the man to be alone. The man was designed to live in relationship to others and could not experience life as God intended until he could share himself with another person. The closer he would come to another person, the more life would take on its true proportions.

The respected author and counselor Larry Crabb confirms this:

> People everywhere long for intimate relationships. We all need to be close to someone. Make no apology for your strong desire to be intimate with someone; it is neither sinful nor selfish. Don't ignore the need by preoccupying yourself with peripheral satisfactions such as social achievement or acquiring knowledge. Neglecting your longing for a relationship by claiming to be above it is as foolish as pretending you can live without food. Our need for relationship is real, and it is there by God's design.[4]

God has built into our soul a need to relate to others. Detached from meaningful relationships, we miss an essential piece of life itself. Seminary professor Michael Wilkins writes, "I am most alive when I am properly connected to what is real. Life involves connectedness with the fullness of reality. The relationships with my wife and children, the enjoyment of creation on a summer morning hike in the mountains with friends — these things connect me to life in such a way that I am *more* alive."[5]

Ultimate Relationship!

The ultimate relationship we were designed for is with God. All other relationships are reflections of this primary one, and all are affected by it. All human relationships have limitations — even the best of them. There is a relational barricade of humanness that cannot be penetrated. But with God, there is no confining boundary. In fact, the only boundaries to intimacy with God are those that *we* impose upon it. Author Oswald Sanders writes, "Both Scripture and experience teach that it is we, not God, who determine the degree of intimacy with Him that we enjoy. We are at this moment as close to God as we really choose to be."[6]

In Sanders's statement, there is both an invitation and an indictment. God beckons us to come ever closer and then holds us

accountable for our choice. We can enjoy the pleasure of God's company or tolerate the effects of spiritual IDS. The seventeenth-century
theologian Blaise Pascal put it this way: "There once was in man a
true happiness of which now remain to him only the mark and empty
trace, which he in vain tries to fill from all his surroundings, seeking
from the things absent the help he does not obtain in things present.
But these are all inadequate, because the infinite abyss can only be
filled by an infinite and immutable object, that is to say, only by
God Himself."[7]

Consider this. The Creator of the universe, whose awesome titles
go on endlessly, gave Moses permission to use God's own personal
name — Yahweh.* Moses was no longer to be a stranger. God desired
an intimate relationship with him, one close enough to hear God's
voice when it was whispered. Such relational turf is described as "holy
ground." It is impossible to leave unchanged from such an encounter
with God.

Moses not only spoke God's personal name, but he heard his own.
There is nothing more personal than your own name. Can you imagine hearing your name spoken by the voice of God? I don't imagine
Moses heard a rumbling thunder reverberating off those jagged rocks.
I can't imagine that his name was spoken with blunt formality. I'm
certain it did not sound distant or condemning. God was not out to
impress Moses with deep, earth-shattering decibels, and God wasn't
trying to drive Moses away. Instead, I'm inclined to think that God
used a tone of voice that communicated a majestic tenderness, a fearful attraction to the Creator. I wonder if that voice sounded much
like that of Jesus.

It Is Who You Know!

Knowing God

Quoting again from Pascal: "There are three kinds of people: those
who have sought God and found him, . . . these are reasonable and
happy; those who seek God and have not yet found him, . . . these are
reasonable and unhappy; and those who neither seek God nor find

---

*I will be using this personal name throughout the book.

him, ... these are unreasonable and unhappy."[8] In terms of intimacy, many believers have sought to come close to God but seem to have not yet experienced standing on that holy ground. I wonder if maybe they have settled for the structure of the Christian life without ever knowing the heat of God's presence, faithfully going through the motions but doing it from a distance. Years ago, I heard a story that captures this idea.

In the fall of 1975, a young man arrived in Michigan after having spent his entire summer studying geography in Israel. He returned home from his travels late on a Saturday evening but was determined to be in church the next morning. After all, the church had paid the entire bill for his learning experience. So early Sunday morning he made his way to the service and sat in the back row of the small auditorium. But the pastor spotted him and invited the young man to sit on the platform throughout the service. They had missed him and wanted to enjoy his presence among them. At the end of the service, the pastor brought the young man to the pulpit and said, "Jim, we have prayed for you all summer. And you know, that was a very expensive trip." As the grateful student attempted to express his appreciation, the pastor continued, "I believe the best way you could thank us would be for you to lead us in a closing prayer ... in Hebrew."

Now, in his ten weeks in Israel, Jim had learned a few Hebrew words but nowhere near enough to pray in that language. It occurred to him, however, that if he didn't pray, maybe these people would want their money back. So he decided to go for it. With his head bowed reverently, Jim began with the words, "Avenu b'shemayim" (our Father in heaven). Then he continued, "Ehad shenayim sheloshah. Arbaah hamishah shishah. Shivah shimonah tishah, ... asarah. Amen." It sounded quite impressive, and a satisfied hush followed the brief prayer as everyone savored what was obviously a very spiritual moment.

As Divine Providence would have it, a Jewish-Christian couple was visiting that church for the very first time that Sunday. After the service, as people were leaving the building and shaking the young man's hand, one of the elderly Jewish believers whispered into the student's ear, "Had you been there another ten weeks, ... eleven, twelve, thirteen." You see, all the tired student had done was to count from one through ten.[9]

Could it be that many believers, feeling the pressure to perform, find themselves living the Christian life "by the numbers"? The mechanics of the Christian life can look very spiritual, no matter who is performing them. But to those who have lived close to the Creator, it is obvious who is really in communion with God and who is just counting. Too many believers seem to have forged the name of God on their spiritual lives. Devoting themselves to the routines of a Christian lifestyle, they may have settled for consistency in place of intimacy. They may know a great deal *about* God, but they may have come short of actually knowing him personally.

Author and theologian J. I. Packer says, "What makes life worthwhile is having a big enough objective, something which catches our imagination and lays hold of our allegiance; and this the Christian has, in a way that no other man has. For what higher, more exalted, and more compelling goal can there be than to know God?"[10] Consider these words from Jeremiah 9:23–24:

> Thus says the LORD, "Let not a wise man boast of his wisdom, and let not the mighty man boast of his might, let not a rich man boast of his riches; but let him who boasts boast of this, that he understands and knows Me."

Knowing Oneself

We have been made in the image of God (Genesis 1:26). The more intimately acquainted we become with God, the more we can begin to understand ourselves. Speaker and author Brennan Manning observed, "It is always true to some extent that we make our images of God. It is even truer that our image of God makes us. Eventually we become like the God we imagine."[11] As we draw closer to God, we gain a more accurate view of who he is. In seeing God more clearly, we see ourselves more accurately as ones created in God's image.

While there may be many ways that we have been fashioned into the image of God, there are three that stand out. First of all, we are like God in that we are primarily spiritual beings. The more we relate to God on a spiritual level, the more we become aware of the fact that our physical body is not what we are all about (yahoo!).

Intimacy places emphasis on the inner person, the spiritual person, the real "me" and the real "you." Paul zeroed in on this reality when he wrote,

> Though our outer man is decaying, yet our inner man is being renewed day by day...we look not at the things which are seen, but at the things which are not seen; for the things which are seen are temporal, but the things which are not seen are eternal. (2 Corinthians 4:16–18)

Not only does the image of God show itself in our spirituality; it is also evident in our personality. Our ability to think and choose and carry on a rational conversation with another person is reflective of the God who formed us. All creativity and the ability to produce beauty are inherited from the Creator. Our emotions — love, joy, and happiness as well as sadness, grief, and anger — are essential characteristics of the personality owned by the Awesome Being after whom we are fashioned. When we shout or sing or laugh or cry, we are in some way an extension of God.

The more intimately we know the one who is the primary generator of our personality, the more we see these elements in their pure form, unmarked and without distortion. As we learn more about the personality of God, we learn more about ourselves.

In addition to spirituality and personality, the image of God is expressed in the area of morality. The concepts of right and wrong, good and evil, have no valid anchor apart from God. Morality is the very character of God played out in human lives. It is only as we know God that concepts of morality make any real sense. In the area of morality, we come face-to-face with just how much damage the image of God can suffer. Our proximity to God reveals how distant our own thoughts and motives can be from his. But it is also in the divine presence that our moral compass is calibrated.

Terrifying Possibilities

Drawing Close to a Holy God

When the high priest would enter the Holy of Holies in the temple, so we are told, a rope would be tied around his ankle. As he stepped behind the curtain and entered into the intimacy of that sacred room, there was the terrifying prospect of standing in the very presence of God. If something went wrong, if God's anger was stirred, if the priest was struck dead, those outside the curtain could simply drag the body out and retreat from the site of the disaster.

Moving nearer to a holy God is a serious notion. We are not one of Yahweh's peers, not on an equal plane with God. Appropriately listed among the terms of endearment is the "fear of the Lord." Those who would approach God must do so with the clear awareness of who this Awesome Being is.

In his book *The Silver Chair*, C. S. Lewis creates a scene in which a little girl named Jill finds herself in the imaginary kingdom of Narnia. She is desperately thirsty and finds a stream of cool water. But there between her and the water lies Aslan, the lion, the symbol of God. The conversation begins with a question,

> *"Are you not thirsty?"*
> *"I'm dying of thirst,"* said Jill.
> *"Then drink,"* said the Lion.
> *"May I — could I — would you mind going away while I do?"* said Jill.
> The lion answered this only by a look and a very low growl. And as Jill gazed at its motionless bulk, she realized that she might as well have asked the whole mountain to move aside for her convenience.
> The delicious rippling noise of the stream was driving her nearly frantic.
> *"Will you promise not to do anything to me if I do come?"* said Jill.
> *"I make no promises,"* said the lion.
> Jill was so thirsty now that, without noticing it, she had come a step nearer.
> *"Do you eat girls?"* she said.
> *"I have swallowed up girls and boys, women and men, kings and emperors, cities and realms,"* said the lion. It didn't say this as if it were boasting, nor as if it were sorry, nor as if it were angry. It just said it.
> *"I daren't come and drink,"* said Jill.
> *"Then you will die of thirst,"* said the lion.
> *"O dear!"* said Jill, coming another step nearer, *"I suppose I must go and look for another stream then."*
> *"There is no other stream,"* said the lion.[12]

Like the Samaritan woman who had tried so many dry wells of intimacy, we find ourselves confronted with the fact that "there is no other stream." The water is real, and the fact that it is within reach only intensifies our thirst. God invites us to drink. But in order to quench our desperate thirst, we must approach the Holy One.

Drawing Close to a Personal God

There are certain frightening aspects to intimacy with a personal God. It entails the risk of exposure and the possibility of rejection. We tend to approach all relationships with caution, jealously guarding our hearts.

Drawing close to a personal God means that we must relate to him on a personal level. Meaningless formalities and repetitious prayers are incompatible with intimacy. Relating on a personal level means that we must communicate personal things. On that personal level there are hopes and dreams, along with fears and insecurities. This type of relating is blatantly honest. It is the type of communication recorded in the Psalms. The end result is that we expose our soul.

Intimacy requires that we relate to God as a person rather than as a faceless force out there somewhere. There is to be conversation with God, rather than repetitious monologues or passing comments. Relating to a person calls for focused attention and meaningful interaction. It involves a long and sustained pursuit. An intimate relationship with God is not available to the casual seeker. It requires a passion of the heart that is all-consuming:

> " 'You will seek me and find me when you seek me with all your heart. I will be found by you.' " (Jeremiah 29:13–14, NIV)

Quite honestly, I would like intimacy to come much easier than it does. I would like it to fit into my current patterns of living. I would like to feel closer to God without having to move from where I am today. I would like a default intimacy that miraculously appears when I mumble a prayer or read a verse from the Bible. When I realize that I have wandered off and messed up my life with some creative expression of sin, I want to be instantly restored without any consequences. I want to be free to replay the prodigal son story over and over again in my life.

The spiritual world is the real world. And in that real world, life does not operate on our terms. More specifically, we do not create the rules for intimacy. If we do not enjoy authentic intimacy with God, could it be that we are the problem? Are we expecting to be close to God on our own terms? Ravi Zacharias confronts this mentality head-on: "Softened as we are by our comforts and by a false idea that serving God is easy and exhilarating, we wonder why He is so far away from us when, in fact, it may be that we are the ones who have left His proximity."[13]

Conclusion: "I Will Be Found by You"

What an amazing statement! God is not hiding from us but is accessible and approachable. When we move closer, God will not withdraw or push us away. Intimacy is not reserved for some exclusive cadre of supersaints who have managed to gain a favored status with God. It is real people like you and me drawing close to the real God of the Bible and experiencing with him a joyful confidence, a gracious understanding, a relaxed presence, a perpetual attraction, and a warm affection.

The ultimate relationship we were designed for is with God, the King of all creation. God longs for us to draw close to him, to enjoy him, to love him. If we move toward him, God's promise is clear: "I will be found by you."

Drawing Closer

1. What is the current state of your relationship with God? Do you feel close to God or distant? Why do you feel that way?

2. Why do you want to draw close to God? How would you describe your desire for spiritual intimacy?

3. Imagine God asking you the questions on page 11. How would you answer those questions?

4. What is your reaction to the quotation from Oswald Sanders on page 13. If it is true, what does it say about your own spiritual life?

5. To what extent is your spiritual life being lived "by the numbers"? Which areas of your relationship with God are seemingly more mechanical than personal?

—⟶ TWO ⟵—

Points of Reference

(pursuing God without getting lost)

R UTHIE AND I LIVED ON THE COAST OF OREGON FOR ABOUT TEN years. I had the privilege of pastoring a wonderfully adventurous body of believers. At least once each month, I would need to travel to Portland, sixty miles away, for various ministry responsibilities. The most direct route was a winding highway through a forested mountain pass, much of it a state park. It was a beautiful but potentially hazardous journey, often complicated by the notorious rain, snow, and fog of the Pacific Northwest.

On one occasion, I made matters even worse by returning home in the dark and traveling an unfamiliar alternate route. Shortly after I began my trip, I encountered a fog thick enough to hide the necessary road signs and landmarks. I locked onto the first tail lights I could find, figuring that anyone else on the road must also have the same destination. As the fog thickened, we slowed our pace, and I moved closer to my guiding lights. We had crept through perhaps a dozen miles of twisted road when our first stop sign brought the procession to a halt. It wasn't until then that I pulled close enough to my leader to read a bumper sticker he had pasted between those tail lights. In simple block letters it warned, "Don't follow me. I'm lost too!"

I felt an odd mixture of humor and dismay as I watched the car turn onto the seemingly unmarked crossroad and vanish into the dense cloud. So now what? I had no idea where I was, no clue in which direction I was pointing, and absolutely no intuitive compulsion to continue straight or try to catch my leader. I wasn't even confident that I could turn around and find my way back to Portland.

21

So I just waited for a new leader to come along. One finally did, and by God's grace I made it home.

It seems that much of my spiritual life resembles that trip home from Portland. As I attempt to make my way home, there are times when I cannot see the spiritual landscape. I am not quite sure where I am or if I am even heading in the right direction. So I wait for someone to come along who looks as if he or she knows the way, and I simply follow — at least for a while. What I really need is a good map and enough visibility to get my bearings. I need to line up my inner compass with true north, get myself pointed in the right direction, and start moving.

The Starting Point

Intimacy with God has a beginning. If you have not begun a relationship with God, you cannot hope to experience intimacy with him. You cannot move closer to someone you have never really met. Although God has chosen to draw people to himself in endless ways, there is a definite starting point to the Christian life. It is a specific place in time, before which one was not saved and after which one was. The Bible makes no reference to some gray area in which one is uncertain about salvation. No one just gradually oozes into a radical life transformation with Christ, and there is no one who has "always been a Christian."

For me, that specific point occurred in the spring of 1969. It began when I accepted an invitation to a youth meeting at a local church. I had sought the friendship of several in that group and saw this as a great opportunity. I heard them talk about the changes God was making in their lives and about the responses to prayer they had experienced. As I continued in the church activities, I began playing a game. Imitating the things I had heard, I invented my own accounts of how God was changing me and answering my prayers. But in reality, there were no changes and no prayers. It's amazing what we will do to be accepted by our peers.

At first I felt the guilt of my dishonesty, but the acceptance it brought was worth whatever price I had to pay. Eventually, I began to believe my own lies. I suppose I had graduated to a full-fledged hypocrite. It wasn't until several years later that I was confronted with reality. I had enlisted in the army for two years and was sent to Fort Lewis, Washington, for basic training. There I was in a barracks with a busload of Hispanics from the streets of San Jose. Now, being six feet two inches with blond hair, I wasn't exactly going to blend into the crowd.

Early on, I made a few feeble attempts at maintaining my Christian facade. I attended a couple of worship services and occasionally mumbled, "Praise the Lord!" However, these tokens now produced the opposite effect. Instead of creating friendships, my actions generated ridicule. It seemed obvious to everyone that my "Christianity" was a sham. By the end of boot camp, I too was convinced.

On my first leave, someone became boldly honest with me. She had watched me for years and wondered when I would grow weary of pretending. One night, after hearing again what Jesus offered to me, I decided it was time to face reality. I prayed, asking Jesus to forgive my sin and to make me the person he had always intended me to be. At that moment, something happened. I was no longer a hypocrite. Honestly admitting my sin and accepting God's gift of forgiveness meant I no longer had to pretend. At the same moment, something else began to happen. All the changes and responses to prayer I had heard about back in those church youth meetings began to take place in my life. I discovered what the Bible means when it says,

> If anyone is in Christ, he is a new creature; the old things passed away; behold, new things have come. (2 Corinthians 5:17)

Before you proceed with this book, it would be good to take a long, hard look at this spiritual pivot point in your own life. Have you dealt honestly and decisively with the issues of salvation? Can you identify a moment in history when you came before God and

- admitted that you were a sinner in need of a savior?
- asked God's forgiveness based on the shed blood of Jesus?
- accepted God's gift of new life in Christ?

Without this vital link to spiritual intimacy, the rest of this book will probably make no sense to you. It will simply be the source of further frustration and discouragement. One can only mature spiritually after he or she has been born spiritually. The evidence of spiritual life can only be produced in those who have that life within them. An honest encounter with the person of Jesus establishes the foundation for building the relationship that is described in the following pages. The focus of this book is on the life of one who has already encountered the Savior and has begun the spiritual adventure known as the Christian life.

The Reference Points

Having established its starting point, we can go on to describe the landscape of an intimate life with God. Three reference points are important to recognize: visibility, attractiveness, and progression.

Visibility

Intimacy with God is visible. You can see it. The Scriptures are filled with descriptive terms and pictures to help us visualize the reality of a new life in Christ. Consider the following verses:

> "Let your light shine before men in such a way that they may see your good works, and glorify your Father who is in heaven." (Matthew 5:16)

> The fruit [visible evidence] of the Spirit is love, joy, peace, patience, kindness, goodness, faithfulness, gentleness, self-control. (Galatians 5:22–23)

> Keep your behavior excellent among the Gentiles, so that . . . they may glorify God because of your good deeds, as they observe them. (1 Peter 2:12)

To portray the visibility of new life in Christ, the Bible uses the imagery of light shining in darkness (Matthew 5:14), fruit appearing on trees (Matthew 7:16–18), and a letter being read by all who come in contact with it (2 Corinthians 3:2–3). The lifestyle of a believer is to be filled with blatant good works that cannot be overlooked by those apart from Christ (1 Peter 2:12). Such is the evidence of a life lived close to God.

Our connectedness to God is to be observable as a showcase of God's grace and mercy and power. A life linked to God shows forth in a high-contrast, countercultural lifestyle. It's not merely the clean-cut look, complete with "church clothes," that distinguishes us. It's not the Christian jargon punctuated with spiritual buzzwords that sets us apart. It's not the church-centered schedule that identifies those who have placed faith in Jesus. The unsaved can do all of these and often do. It is, instead, the qualities of a changed heart that signal the presence of new life. Ambrose Bierce, a cynical commentator, described it in newspaper terminology: "A saint is a dead sinner, revised and edited."

I once heard a Romanian believer describe what he had experienced during the days of heavy oppression and persecution in his home country. Romanian Christians could not speak openly about their faith, so these believers had to live lives that were so visibly different that they demanded an explanation. But it should not require persecution to force us to live such visibly different lives.

Formless faith. We have a tendency to gravitate toward the theoretical and philosophical, toward concepts and principles. It is safer there. The Christian life is far less intimidating when viewed as a concept. As long as we don't define it, we don't have to *do* anything with it. It is much easier to pass it off when it is left a bit vague and out of reach for the average person. When biblical principles aren't translated into practical applications and concepts aren't nailed down into doable deeds, the new life within a believer remains formless. Is it any wonder that we find ourselves in such a spiritual fog?

If God has authentically made someone a new person in Christ, it will be detectable by others. It will not be something accomplished in secret, deep within the private chambers of one's soul and never exposed to the light of day. It is life that is open for public inspection. Galatians 5:22–23 lists nine observable traits of the spiritual life, while 2 Peter 1:5–7 compiles a sequence of seven. Combining these with a host of individually mentioned qualities results in the portrait of a life characterized by practical discernment, an optimistic spirit, and other-centered activities. I have chosen to focus attention on five specific qualities of the spiritual life: relational impact, downsized ego, serious laughter, applied potential, and encoded ethics. These qualities are developed in part 3. They may sound a bit foreign to those familiar with the Scriptures and accustomed to more traditional terminology. If so, great! I desire to aerate our thinking and revitalize how we visualize ourselves in Christ.

Attractiveness

Intimacy with God is attractive. Every quality listed in the Scriptures is one that is desirable, positive, and beneficial. They are features that others notice because they are uncommon. People are drawn to these qualities because they are what we truly want. There are certain things we long for in the core of our being. We may not be able to put these passions into words, but we still pursue them. I believe that people don't really know what they want until they see it. But when they do see it, something lights up inside them, and they will do whatever they can to get it.

I see this in myself. I know that I am drawn to people who are not pretending to be something they are not. I can't help but notice those who are unselfish and have compassion for others. I enjoy being around people who put a positive spin on life and who have learned to recognize the hand of God in their life. I am attracted to those who bring life to life. It has been said that a saint is one who makes it easy for others to believe. I often wonder how easy I make it for those around me or if I tend to leave them in a fog.

Progression

Spiritual life is progressive. There is no such thing as instant intimacy with God. None of its qualities mysteriously appear in one's life overnight. It is produced, not by default, but by design and is the result of specific, consistent, ongoing decisions in the daily life of a believer — decisions that draw the presence of authentic life to the surface. As a result, the longer one knows Christ and matures in a relationship with him, the more attractive one's life should become.

It has been duly noted that the only evidence of life is growth and the only evidence of growth is change. If life runs rampant within us, then it would seem that luxuriant growth and widespread changes would naturally accompany it. Second Peter 1:8 says, "If these qualities are yours and are increasing, they render you neither useless nor unfruitful." In 1 Thessalonians 4:1, after applauding the state of their spiritual life, Paul challenges those believers to "excel still more." The progressive nature of our relationship with God is limitless. It is a process that continues to our dying breath.

Everything takes time. I belong to a very exclusive club. It's the I-wore-braces-on-my-teeth-as-an-adult club. Wisdom teeth (who came up with that name?) had crowded my lower teeth, and a missing molar had allowed my upper teeth to drift. As a result, my mouth was a mess, my jaw was out of alignment, and I was facing some serious speech problems if I did not take some corrective action.

The whole experience was an illustration of the Christian life. The day my teeth were wired together, my whole mouth went into shock. Although I was convinced that I had done the right thing, I also knew that there would be some rough days ahead. Every time those wires were retied, I felt tension and pain. About the time I was getting used to the adjustment, it was time for another retie. Everything related to my mouth felt unnatural. It was almost like learning to speak and eat all over again. The long process was punctuated with only small incremental changes visible each month.

Authentic spiritual maturity is a long, and often painful, process. Real changes always come with a price tag. The more significant the change, the bigger the price. In 2 Peter, the qualities of spiritual maturity are preceded by a very important phrase, "in your faith supply" (1:5). The word translated "supply" means "to provide at your own cost." It is a term that implies responsibility and focused effort. It is an instruction that carries a price tag.

The Contact Points

It was back in the late 1800s that Californians first earned the reputation for making outrageous statements. Greedy real estate brokers were out to make a killing. They figured that if they could just entice people to come out west and experience that beautiful state, no one could resist buying a piece of it. The state was touted as a paradise with a tropical climate that had miraculous effects. A couple of notable attempts to accomplish such enticement ended in fiascoes. The first was in Los Angeles in 1881. Boosters launched a massive promotion for a newspaper editors' convention. They planned it to occur in the dead of winter, boasting that the city had perfect weather year-round. However, a freak storm coincided with the event. One evening, the attendees stepped out of their hotels to find icicles hanging from the lampposts and snow at their feet. The visiting reporters lambasted Californians as liars and swindlers.[1]

It took eleven years to recover from the embarrassment. But in April of 1892, another attempt was made to lure people to the West Coast. This time the realtors sponsored the annual convention for the National Editorial Association. Again, they promoted on a grand scale. It paid off, as thousands arrived for the convention, but this time a heat wave settled in and cooked the trusting tourists. The reporters were merciless in their ridicule. "If it is that hot in the winter," they scoffed, "can you image the intensity of their summers?"[2]

In spite of these promotional bombs, people still poured into California. Arriving on the docks, they were often met by swarms of real estate hustlers. Before these new prospects could get their bearings, they would be ushered to a buggy for a tour of "prime" investment properties. There were often bands playing and barbecues to accompany the tour. Some unscrupulous realtors even tied oranges on Joshua trees, so attempting to sell desert lots as citrus groves.[3]

In our attempts to "sell" Christianity, we may appear as religious hucksters, hawking our spiritual merchandise with questionable advertising and fraudulent claims. We declare that Jesus gives us a better life. But better, by definition, means different. Therefore, if our life is not "different," we cannot contend that it is "better." Friedrich Nietzsche, a fiery German critic, once confronted Christians with the indictment, "If you want me to believe in your Redeemer, you are going to have to act a lot more redeemed." That seems reasonable to me, but how does one act redeemed? What does redemption look like? When the Christian life is fleshed out in the practical dramas of daily living, how is it different from the lives around it?

As believers in Jesus Christ, we claim to have these answers. We boast of having a personal relationship with the one who is life itself and an inside track on how to cope with the issues that have confronted every human who has ever walked the face of this earth. We challenge those around us with a bold announcement that if they would only place their faith in Jesus, he would transform their lives and make them new people.

I believe that all these claims are absolutely true. However, as

I look for the evidence, I am confronted with a frustrating reality. While many allege to have trusted Christ to forgive their sin and remove their guilt, few have ventured on to discover the wonders of a transformed life. The beloved pastor Richard Halverson writes that the "harmless caricature that so often passes for Christianity has failed so completely to impress the world that it rarely if ever occurs to thoughtful men, wrestling with insuperable problems, to take Jesus Christ seriously in terms of a solution."[4]

Theology professor David Needham wishes he could shout a certain statement around the world. "Mark this," he writes, "a Christian is a person who has become someone he was not before."[5] But how do you identify such a new person? What marks should be present in the life of anyone who truly knows Jesus? What form does spiritual life take in the hectic schedule of a young mother? How does it affect the business practices of an executive? How is it lived out on a high-school campus? What does it look like in the life of a career single or a professional athlete or a mechanic or a grandparent? I have lost track of how many times I have asked the following question over the past few years. It amazes me how difficult it has been for believers to answer it. What does an authentic Christian life look like, not in theory, but in practice?

Challenging Self

It is vital that we, as believers, be able to identify authentic spiritual maturity. First of all, it is crucial to one's own personal walk with Christ. Unless we can accurately visualize in practical terms what it looks like to live ever closer to God, we have no way of assessing our spiritual health or the progress of our spiritual journey.

When our first child was born, Ruthie and I subscribed to a monthly newsletter that helped us through the first year of parenting. Each month we would gain insights concerning what to watch for in our child as she matured. It gave plenty of latitude for the differences in the growth rates of children, but we found that information a valuable forecast of her development.

If a child is developing at a normal pace, a parent can relax in the assurance that the child is healthy. But if a parent knows that some characteristic should be emerging by a certain age and it doesn't appear, that parent has reason to be concerned. If a child is not growing physically, we take action. The same is true if a child is not growing mentally or emotionally. We recognize these failures to mature as abnormal and in need of corrective measures. This is exactly what Paul did in addressing the Corinthian believers. It had been scarcely three years since the church had been established, yet Paul reprimanded them for their lack of visible maturity (1 Corinthians 3:1–4).

A certain confidence accompanies the development of spiritual intimacy. It is the confirmation that we really do have new life within us. If we seldom see the evidence of it, we begin to question its existence. In order to instill this confidence in believers of the early church, Peter put together a list of visible marks of spiritual life and then wrote, "Be all the more diligent to make certain about His calling and choosing you" (2 Peter 1:10). The key to this assurance was in the phrase that followed his charge, "as long as you practice these things."

There is also the fact that if we are not moving forward in our spiritual life, we are most certainly moving backward. If we don't move deeper into the Christian life (closer to God), we are doomed to fight border skirmishes the rest of our life. The body of Christ is filled with so many who seem content to live near the line that divides the old life from the new. Gazing back into their former life, they find themselves constantly battling the same issues and never moving past them. Personal growth creates distance between us and our old life.

Choosing Mentors

Secondly, a clear picture of spiritual maturity is vital in the selection of our spiritual heroes, those models and mentors we allow to shape our lives. I once heard Warren Wiersbe say, "Tell who your heroes are and I will write your biography." Author Fred Smith quotes Socrates as saying, "Talk, young man, that I might know you," and then writes that the philosopher could have also added, "Talk of your heroes that I might not only know who you are, but who you will become."[6] Our heroes, our mentors, are those who live the life we want to live. Dick Keyes, in his book, *True Heroism*, describes a hero as "a person who lives out the things that we prize or value most, enough so that we want to emulate that person."[7]

My personal heroes have been drawn from the Bible, history, and personal relationships. In the biblical realm, my heroes include people like Jabez, who broke the pattern of failure in his family and dared to dream God-sized dreams (1 Chronicles 4:9–10). David is also one of them, as he cultivated a heart for God that combined the creativity of a musician with the passion of a warrior.

From history, one of my heroes is Count Nikolaus Ludwig von Zinzendorf, who led the believers of an embattled, self-centered church into one of the greatest missionary movements. I am also fascinated by Martin Luther, who rebelled against inauthentic Christianity and put his life on the line.

Then, for me, the list also includes a neighbor woman who faithfully prayed for me each day of my high-school years and my aunt who took the time to confront me with my spiritual condition. It includes a pilot in Vietnam who used flying as a classroom to patiently teach me the basics of the Christian life and a pastor who made God's Word come alive for me. There is my father-in-law, who provided me with a model for ministry, and a retired woman who launched virtually every creative ministry for which I received credit in my ten years on the coast of Oregon.

One other vital reason for identifying the works of spiritual maturity is for our selection of leaders within the body of Christ. If these are to be model believers who set the pace for others, and if they are to be those who determine the vision for a ministry and make decisions that affect the course of that ministry, these must be individuals who are genuinely in pursuit of intimacy with God. In his book *The Effective Church Board*, Michael Anthony observes, "Although much has been written by Christian authors on the subject of leadership styles, I find relatively few passages in Scripture that deal with this topic as it relates to the church. However, the Bible is filled with references to the character qualities of an effective leader."[8]

The Scriptures detail a number of visible qualities of spiritual maturity that must be present in anyone who would endeavor to lead God's people. Passages like 1 Timothy 3:1–13 and Titus 1:5–9 do not merely provide checklists for those who apply for positions on the church "power team." Instead, they are descriptions of spiritual maturity. The idea is that spiritual leaders are to be growing believers with "life" written all over them.

Among the mentors in my life was Bruce Ker, a former missionary, instructor, and director of a mission organization. I remember listening to a long account of his experience with wonderful opportunities followed by painful disappointments. I have never forgotten his conclusion: "God is infinitely more concerned about me as an individual than he is about anything I will ever do." That statement has been a driving force in my life for many years now. I am convinced of its truth.

God desires to attract others by drawing us close and by putting his life on display in us. When it comes to the bottom line, it is not what we do but who we are that makes the difference. It is not a self-reformed life that is impressive to those around us; it is a God-transformed life that demands explanation. Author Buell Kazee wrote, "We can never make a *convicting* appeal to this lost world on what we can do for God. But when we go telling and showing what our God has done for us, the world will listen." He goes on to explain the power of a transformed life: "The people around will be impressed with our God; they will never be impressed with us."[9]

It is not my intention to discourage believers by holding up portraits of "perfect" Christians or by outlining some complicated procedure for drawing close to God. I believe there are two reasons why many abandon the pursuit of spiritual intimacy. On the one hand, they simply see it as an impossibility. It's not real life. On the other, many consider it an innate feature of life — either you have or you don't have.

It is also not my intention to confuse natural qualities with those that are produced by the Spirit of God. The natural characteristics of one individual's personality cannot be reproduced in someone else. Using what comes naturally to one person as a pattern for another is unreasonable, unfair, and unbiblical. The elements of spiritual maturity identified in this book are those that come as a result of a life-transforming relationship with Jesus. They are each exciting, realistic possibilities for any and every person who knows the Savior. They are, in fact, expected in all who claim new life in Christ.

Every mark of spiritual intimacy was lived out in Jesus. People loved him. They were drawn to him, not because of spoken truth alone, but because Jesus lived that truth in practical terms that made everyday routines come alive. It was life as they had never seen it before, bringing texture to truth. Jesus embodied authentic life, free from the defeating, dysfunctional features of sin. Everything they had been taught about God was fleshed out in the daily life of Jesus. It was seen in his actions and expressions, heard in his stories and laughter, and felt in the touch of his hand.

The same life Jesus put on display is what he offers to those who have entered into a faith relationship with him. That life is the tangible proof of the statement made by Irenaeus back in the second century, "The glory of God is man fully alive."[10] Too many are willing to settle for a bored and lifeless existence when they could be "fully alive."

Conclusion

As a young couple attending graduate school in Portland, Oregon, Ruthie and I would look for inexpensive (key word) entertainment. One Saturday morning, we noticed a newspaper announcement for a ship launching. That sounded interesting. It was open to the public and included a free luncheon, so off we went.

Arriving at the shipyard, we were met with an impressive sight. A giant oil tanker sat on the banks of the Willamette River, prepared for a sideways launching. After officials offered a prayer and some brief remarks of great expectations, the ship was christened the G.T. *Chevron Colorado*. A cheesecloth-wrapped champagne bottle crashed against its hull, and the vessel began to thunder down a short ramp into the water. There were cheers and confetti and horn blasts as the *Colorado* plunged into its new environment. A squadron of bull-nose tugs were on hand to stabilize the ship and move it to its next location.

When the noise began to die down and people started moving toward the food, I asked one of the more official-looking men when the *Colorado* would take its maiden voyage. I was surprised to learn that it would still be quite awhile. "It still needs to be outfitted," he said. "It may look complete from the outside, but there is still quite a bit that must be done on the inside before it is ready for service."

After a believer is launched into a new life with Christ, there is still work that must be done inside. It is a spiritual "outfitting" with the basic qualities of a normal Christian life. In contrast to the *Colorado*, this outfitting *does* affect our appearance. These qualities are visible, attractive, and progressive.

Drawing Closer

1. Take some time to put your spiritual starting point in writing. How and when did you place your faith in Jesus Christ and begin your personal relationship with God?

2. What do you believe an authentic Christian life looks like? What character qualities should be emerging, and what spiritual skills should be developing?

3. What benefits can one experience from having a spiritual mentor? Do you have one? If not, how would you go about finding one? What would you look for in such a person?

4. How is God currently "outfitting" your spiritual life? What part does spiritual intimacy play in this process?

5. What do you believe others say about God as a result of being with you? What would you want them to say?

THREE

Facts of Life

(looking for God without getting discouraged)

F LYING ON A MAJOR AIRLINE CAN BE QUITE AN EXPERIENCE. I AM always pleasantly relieved to find I have been assigned a seat with enough legroom to accommodate my six-foot, two-inch frame, much of which is legs. On one flight a few years ago, my wife and I were seated on the aisle in the first row of the coach section. I had plenty of room to stretch my legs and no seat in front of me to drop back and encroach upon my knee space. My location, however, wasn't notable for legroom alone; it had a couple of additional features.

Seated on the aisle, I had a perfect window into the posh world of first-class flying. That feature allowed me to have fun watching another world. But the other feature of the seating location can be a nightmare. Where my wife and I sat is the row most frequently requested by mothers with small children. Seated across the aisle from me, as evidence of this pattern and as potential proof of Murphy's Law, was a young mother with her two cute children — a two-year-old and an infant. I began adjusting my expectations.

I must say that this mother handled the situation with calm and gracious expertise. What was even more impressive, however, was the loving care and attention provided to this family by our flight attendant. From the earliest moments of the journey, she anticipated their every need, and with warm smiles and kind words, she seemed to enjoy her servant role. She was actually having fun!

By stark contrast, I watched a different story unfolding in first class. A well-dressed and perfectly groomed flight attendant was going about similar tasks with those in the leather seats, but it was obvious that she was not enjoying herself. Although she smiled at each passenger, a certain distance to her expression stole its authenticity. The curtain between the two compartments had not been drawn, and she was unaware that she was being observed. As the flight progressed, she became visibly bothered by the needs of those around her.

There may have been many legitimate reasons to account for the attendant's weariness and distance, but the contrast was amazing. Something needed to be said, not to the bothered attendant, but to the one who had made our experience so pleasant by her attitude and her actions. So, near the end of the flight, we caught her attention for a moment. We told her how much we appreciated what she had done for that mother and how encouraging it was to see her enjoying what she was doing. To accentuate our point, we called attention to her coworker who was having such a hard day.

"She's a senior flight attendant," she said softly. "They all tend to get that way."

We talked briefly about how long she had been working for the airlines and asked about her plans for the future. Her response was not what we expected. She glanced quickly toward the expensive seats and leaned a bit closer to us.

"You know, I really enjoy what I do, but in a couple more years I will qualify as a senior flight attendant. At that time, I plan to find something else to do. I don't want to become like her."

I believe we are always in danger of cultivating a generation of "senior flight attendant" Christians, a generation of believers who are polished in their appearance and in the routines of church life, believers who provide the appropriate answers with a smile and who are genuinely loyal to the Kingdom but who are in desperate need of something vital to their very identity. Something powerful is missing — something that makes younger believers long to grow in Christ, something that continuously renews the excitement of our spiritual adventure, something that confirms the reality of new life in Christ. I believe that "something" is intimacy with God.[1]

It would seem that it should not be that difficult to find a mentor among those who claim to know Jesus. Churches should comprise people whose lives have been changed and are continuing to change, becoming increasingly more like the Savior-King they follow — not perfect people but refreshingly real people who are living lives that are different, people who are genuinely growing and maturing in their relationship with Christ, authentic models of what the Redeemer desires to accomplish in everyone who comes to him. However, authentic signs of life can be sparse.

Now there may be many legitimate reasons for the lack of visible marks of spiritual maturity in a particular believer on a certain day or in a specific setting. Many of those we find in a growing church are simply at a point of searching for answers. They do not yet possess new life. Others are still rookies, learning the basics of new life in Christ. Some are wrestling with how to respond to the latest "opportunity" life has presented to them. Some are in pain; some are scared; some are confused. But even accounting for a portion of unbelievers and new believers and giving room for an unusually rough day for others, the pattern among God's people should be one of unmistakable life. Why is this missing in so many who identify themselves with the Redeemer?

Intimate Distortions

Many books in Christian bookstores today revile the church for its weaknesses and failures; many caustic pages highlight what is wrong. It is relatively easy to point out what has gone haywire; the average person in any church does it all the time. So with such a great volume of material available to identify the spiritual problems of our day, you may not be looking forward to another whack at the church. I can understand that, but I believe there are certain facts of life, spiritual life, that must be faced.

Spiritual realities must be distinguished from false assumptions. I realize that in coming nose to nose with them, some readers may feel an understandable defensiveness. But please be assured that it is not my intention to grind an ax or attack any particular segment of the body of Christ. However, it is my belief that if something needs to be corrected, the first step is to identify it as a problem. So when it comes to spiritual intimacy, if we have been operating with an unbiblical model driven by false assumptions, we must first recognize the flaws before we can proceed to alter our course. With that in mind, please consider with me what I believe are five distortions of spiritual intimacy prevalent in churches today.

Distortion 1: Longevity

The longer we know God, the closer we will come to God. As explained in chapter 2, the longer one knows Jesus, the more attractive that person's life *should* become. But unfortunately spiritual growth, unlike its physical counterpart, never happens by default. It is a sad reality that one can know the Savior for a lifetime and still remain an entry-level believer.

Churches are filled with those who have settled in for the duration. Studies continually reveal that the majority of any congregation is willing to sit back and wait for heaven. A weekly dose of well-crafted worship and a garnish of social interaction with a few like-minded church people sum up the spiritual life of most American Christians. Sitting in a pew week after week, one is bound to absorb some truth, but over the years "attending" church can become just another habit — not a bad habit but just one of those ruts of life that do little more than divert our attention for a few hours. It is easy to develop a habit of listening to truth rather than responding to it, of taking notes and never becoming living fulfillments of the Word, of being in the presence of God but never encountering the Presence.

Mothball fleet. One of the first times I ventured north of San Francisco, it was across the Carquinez Bridge. I was presented with an impressive sight: an armada of ships, anchored port to starboard. I became a road hazard as I gazed at hundreds of vintage warships, proud evidence of U.S. military strength. This was one of the Navy's "mothball" fleets.

Constructed during World War II, the majority of these vessels bore such proud names as Liberty ships and Victory ships. They were designed to carry the very life of battle within them. Interestingly, most of these particular ships had never seen action. Their only voyage had been from the shipbuilding yard to this obscure bay. Each had been assigned a location and had been well maintained for the span of a generation. They were spotless and fully equipped, but only a few had ever experienced the purpose for which they were made. In the years that followed my first sighting of this fleet, I watched the numbers dwindle. One by one, they were sold as barges or dismantled for scrap. Their years of "service" having ended, they were being returned to the shipyards.

Having designed us with an awesome purpose in mind, God intends for us to sail the open seas into the heat of spiritual battle, carrying Life within us. We are spiritual Victory ships and Liberty ships. God owns no mothball fleets. While longevity provides the opportunity to mature in our relationship with God, it does not guarantee it. In fact, if one does not grow, the years actually foster a disillusionment, a lowering of expectations to match an empty experience.

Disappointed believers may continue to be very polite and polished in their appearance. They may move through the routines of church life with graceful ease, but something is missing.

I will be found by you...

I long to draw you close and bless you with the warmth of my presence. Time alone will not provide this. If you do not capture my presence in the eternity of each moment, time will simply become the space that defines your boredom. I have not intended for you to live a sedentary spirituality.[2]

Distortion 2: Historicity

What we have done in the past determines our relationship with God today. Living on the basis of past accomplishments can provide another occasion for misreading maturity in one's walk with Christ. While a history of faithful service to the Master can provide a solid foundation for one's present walk, spiritual maturity and the intimacy that accompanies it cannot be stored away. In fact, the moment we stop moving closer to God is the moment our spiritual life begins to deteriorate.

Spiritual folklore. I find it exciting to read about believers who have put their lives on the line to serve our great God. First Kings 18 tells the story of one such man. Obadiah smuggled about a hundred preachers out from under the nose of a murderous dictator. He hid them in a remote cave and fed them at his own expense until the danger had passed. Obadiah's courageous "underground" rescue was carried out so perfectly that the powerful leaders of the bloody regime never discovered what happened. In subsequent years, the daring adventures of this brave young believer were recounted with glorious detail in the private lamplight of God-fearing homes. I am certain that Obadiah himself enjoyed giving his own firsthand account of those times, and he probably never lacked an audience.

However, in that long period of time following the heroic deeds, there was seemingly more talk of what had happened in the past than there were current happenings about which to talk. This was true until a fiery new preacher came to town and challenged Obadiah to put his life on the line once again. Now Obadiah was much older, in the more graceful and definitely more respected years of his life. His initial response was to simply remind this young preacher that he had always feared God and had a faithful past, which had even become folklore in his own lifetime. It was time for someone else to be brave.

I have heard many exciting stories of the past. Often, when I visit in homes or have guests in our home, I will hear firsthand accounts of how believers have served our mighty God in former times. The stories can be as rich with the pulse of the Spirit as are the pages of Scripture itself. Many are filled with joy and excitement, adventure and victory. God has been at work among his people.

The sad fact, however, is that most of these people are from the same tribe as Obadiah. Their past experiences have not translated into the present. In the years when they should have the most effective ministry of their life, they sit spiritually idle. The thrill of serving in close proximity to our glorious God is only a memory. The Adversary is more than willing to concede past defeats if it means that spiritual warriors will simply retire their sword over the fireplace mantle and reminisce their remaining years away. Spiritual intimacy takes place only in the present.

The "senior flight attendant" syndrome has a tendency to sneak up on a believer. Without ever noticing the subtle changes, one can begin to talk more in the past tense than in the present. A well-deserved honor is rightly attached to those spiritual accomplishments of the past, but life moves on, and something is missing.

I *will* be found by you...

I am seeking more than the memory of our past adventures together. I want our relationship to preoccupy your mind and fascinate your heart ...today. I have so much more of me to offer you, and there is so much more of you to reveal.[3]

Distortion 3: Activity

Our service for the Kingdom determines our closeness to the King. While involvement can be a valid expression of one's spiritual health, it can also be a way of evading the real issues of encountering God. Jesus once reprimanded a close friend for being too busy. She was serving him! Her name was Martha, the sister of Lazarus and Mary, a resident of Bethany. "Martha, Martha, you are worried and bothered about so many things," he told her, "only a few things are necessary, really only one" (Luke 10:41–42). Even those with good intentions can become more concerned about the activities of the Kingdom than about the King.

In many churches, activity is the measure of spiritual maturity. The more involved one becomes, the more spiritual points that person gains. Committees, Sunday school classes, choir, seasonal activities, and special projects all count. Eventually, one can win the ultimate prize of being at church every time the doors are unlocked. Yahoo!

Overactivity is more often a clue that something is wrong rather than right. Remember those words from Bruce Ker, "God is infinitely more concerned about me as an individual than he is about anything I will ever do." Drawing close to God is not accomplished by performing for him. While Martha's busyness was chided, her sister was praised for her inactivity. Mary sat on holy ground when she nestled at the feet of her Savior-Friend. Jesus weighed the situation in terms of spiritual value and spoke these gentle words, "Mary has chosen what is better, and it will not be taken away from her" (Luke 10:42, NIV).

Perhaps we all find ourselves admiring those who are busy up to their eyeballs accomplishing the work of the Kingdom. Their faithfulness and dedication to the task are to be admired, even praised. For many believers, however, service has become an obligation to be performed by the genuinely loyal. There is a weariness in their service; something is missing.

I *will* be found by you...

I desire your presence as much as you desire mine. I will wait for you in the quiet places, those places where you can best hear my voice, so I will not have to speak over the rumble of your busyness.[4]

Distortion 4: Knowledge

The more we know about God, the closer we are to God. The reasoning that drives this misconception is simple. Putting God's Word into our heads is the same as putting it into our hearts. Therefore, it is thought, the more we know of the Scriptures, the more we grow in our relationship with God. In reality a subtle intellectualizing of Christianity reduces it to facts and drains away its vitality.

In 1988, I received a surprising gift — an all-expense-paid trip to Israel, compliments of the Israeli government. In an effort to increase tourism, they were offering a two-week excursion to a number of pastors. I was one of them. It was first-class all the way, including our guide. He was not only a very enjoyable person, but he was a wealth of information. He knew the Scriptures, Old Testament and New, having memorized much of them. He knew his history very well and was an authority on the archaeological excavations currently underway throughout the country. He genuinely knew what he was talking about and could match wits with any of us in the group. However, although he knew what the Bible said as well as any of us did and had been leading tours with evangelical believers for over twenty-five years, our guide had never given his life to the Messiah. He had successfully confined all this information to the intellectual corridors of his mind, never allowing it to intrude upon his personal life.

Many believers are only one step beyond that tour guide. Having responded to the biblical information about sin and salvation by receiving God's gift of new life in Christ, they have not continued to apply what they know. They may consistently attend worship services, Sunday school classes, and Bible studies. They may have memorized much of the Scriptures and may give some of the best answers to spiritual questions. They may even be the ones leading the classes. But even with all of this, something is missing.

I *will* be found by you...

I long for you to know me, not just information about me, not just the evidence of my involvement throughout history. I have shared with you my personal thoughts to bring you inside my heart.[5]

Distortion 5: Legality

Rigid rules are the gauge of relational intimacy. Seeing a believer living a highly structured life can be appealing, particularly to someone whose life has been out of control. There is a sense of security that comes with clearly defined boundaries. For some, a confining code for living is what keeps them a safe distance from known personal weaknesses. For others, it protects them from fear of the unknown. The wide-open ranges of freedom can be intimidating.

We all have a need to set some personal boundaries based upon what we know about ourselves. But those personal restrictions are not necessarily evidence of spiritual progress. They tend to dilute the declaration, "It was for freedom that Christ set us free" (Galatians 5:1).

A life of legalism can have the appearance of living by a "higher standard." Yet of all the practices that Jesus repulsed, this was the one he attacked with the greatest ferocity. It was captured best in a group of conservatives known as the Pharisees. They lived lives of meticulous accuracy, committed to obeying the Scriptures. They were clean-cut, respectable believers — model citizens. Yet some of Jesus' most scathing remarks were pointed at them and their rigid legalism.

Some of the characteristics of legalism reveal how deadly this form of inauthenticity can be. For example, it is more often about personal preferences than it is about biblical mandates. Legalism always involves a list of dos and don'ts, mainly don'ts, and is marked by pettiness and trivia, missing the main points of the gospel. Legalism is usually driven by an angry spirit, rather than by love, and places an emphasis on the mechanics of living over the condition of the heart. Demanding that others conform to a prescribed lifestyle, and that they do it now, legalism is ultimately a relationship to a standard, more than it is to a Savior.

Could it be that we are in too much of a rush to make the Christian life look good? Is it possible that in our attempts to show how Jesus has changed our lives, we simply try to conform to a uniform pattern? Living by a set of rules, even biblical rules, may give the appearance of spiritual intimacy, but in the midst of the regimentation, something is missing.

I *will* be found by you...

I yearn for you to venture deeper into my heart. I want you to discover more of the mystery of who I am and who you are in relation to me. I invite you to be my personal friend without any stiff formalities and confining boundaries.[6]

Intimate Consequences

Certain unavoidable consequences attach themselves to the pursuit of something other than authentic spiritual intimacy. If you follow the wrong map, you end up at the wrong destination, someplace where you never intended to go. It can be more than simply discouraging. It can cost you the very core of your spiritual vitality, your sense of connectedness with God. There are three tragic consequences that should be clearly identified and carefully considered. Operating under distortions of spiritual intimacy results in dishonesty with God, distance from God, and disappointment with God.

Consequence 1: Dishonesty with God

When we fail to develop genuine intimacy with God, we commit ourselves to an inauthentic spiritual life. We may still go through the motions expected of a Christian, but we end up dishonest with God and impersonating life. Larry Crabb writes,

Most of us make it through life with some level of stability because we refuse to think about troubling things going on within us. We just keep on keeping on, stifling that nagging sense that something's wrong, that there has to be more. We want to think we've found the key to life, that now we can manage, that our empty heart is filled, that our struggle against sin is now a march of victory. But in order to maintain that happy conviction we must insulate ourselves against the feedback of others who find us still unloving, and we must stubbornly deny the evidence in our soul that more is wrong than we know how to handle. Denial for many becomes a way of life. And years of practice make it possible to seal off from our awareness any data that contradicts what we want to believe. It's frighteningly easy to become deluded about our spiritual maturity.[7]

Consequence 2: Distance from God

When we are dishonest with God, we experience a distance from him. More than just a feeling of vacant space between us, it is a way of living that makes our relationship formal, mechanical, and guarded. Despite our best efforts, it comes off unattractive and inauthentic.

Behind the facade of inauthenticity looms the flesh, a mode of operation that fills any space in our lives that is not consciously put under the control of the Spirit. The composite picture of the flesh has, at its core, a sense of self-importance and a disrespect for authority. Life in the flesh yields a deceptive maneuvering for power that includes the secret whisperings meant to discredit or destroy the reputation of others. A displeasure builds within us at seeing someone else possess what we don't have. There is a quarrelsome disposition that actually desires to harm others, a smoldering anger within, waiting for an opportunity to be expressed, a desperate search for something to deaden the pain. Life in the flesh involves moral and ethical compromises. We find ourselves living like "mere mortals," like those who know nothing of new life in Christ.

Distance from God ends up being played out in life among God's people. Instead of putting on display our closeness to God in terms of love for each other, we demonstrate our distance from him in terms of relational dysfunction. In a book about ministering with such people in the body of Christ, author Marshall Shelley refers to them as well-intentioned dragons:

> Dragons, of course, are fictional beasts, monstrous reptiles with lion's claws, a serpent's tail, bat wings, and scaly skin. They exist only in the imagination.
>
> But there are dragons of a different sort, decidedly real. In most cases, though not always, they do not intend to be sinister; in fact, they're usually quite friendly. But their charm belies their power to destroy.

Within the church, they are often sincere, well-meaning saints, but they leave ulcers, strained relationships, and hard feelings in their wake. They don't consider themselves difficult people. They don't sit up nights thinking of ways to be nasty. Often they are pillars of the community — talented, strong personalities, deservedly respected — but for some reason, they undermine the ministry of the church. They are not naturally rebellious or pathological; they are loyal church members, convinced they're serving God, but they wind up doing more harm than good.[8]

Consequence 3: Disappointment with God

When our definition of the Christian life speaks more to the issues of having the right information and doing the right things, then we have set ourselves up for some serious disappointment, discouragement, and disillusionment. In author Phil Yancey's words, "it happens to ordinary Christians: first comes disappointment, then a seed of doubt, then a response of anger or betrayal. We begin to question whether God is trustworthy, whether we can really stake our lives on him."[9]

Disappointment is the unavoidable result of expecting God to bless a life built around good things that are not intended to move us closer to him or that are not the direct result of a vital, growing relationship with him. After having heard about all the wonderful things God has in store for us, we may begin to wonder what happened to all of those "precious and magnificent promises." Where is the sense of purpose and fulfillment and adventure? Why do we not feel the spiritual power and experience the personal transformation the Bible describes? Is this all there is?

Empty Boxes

Years ago, I heard a story (obviously fiction) about a man who died and was being given a tour of heaven. The angel giving the tour was very thorough, pointing out the rapturous beauty of the landscape and explaining the purpose of each beautiful building they passed. At one point, the angel made a very obvious omission. Gliding around a large white building, the spirit-guide made no comment about its purpose. In fact, it seemed to ignore the structure's very existence. This piqued the curiosity of the newcomer, but when he inquired about it, he was simply told that he would find out soon enough.

As the tour progressed, the white building repeatedly came into view. The man would point to it and ask again what it was. But each time the angel would pass the question off as inappropriate or insignificant. Finally, the man reached a frustration overload (if that is possible in heaven) and demanded an explanation. The angel acquiesced but warned that he might not like what he found.

The entrance was cut through a giant pearl that was shaped like a teardrop. Once inside, they stood in what seemed like a vast warehouse. There was row upon row of white boxes. Each was the size of a steamer trunk, and they were stacked to the ceiling. The man noticed that every box had a person's name printed on it, so he asked if there was one with *his* name. "Of course," the angel replied flatly. "Every citizen of the Kingdom has one."

The man searched until he found the box with his name embossed with gold letters upon it. Fortunately, it was within reach. He drew it from the column and was about to open it when the angel touched his arm and spoke. "I must warn you, royal heir, that what you find within this box may bring you pain beyond what you can bear."

That seemed impossible to the man. He couldn't imagine anything that could bring him pain in heaven. But before needlessly subjecting himself to something that might diminish his new experience, he hesitated long enough to ask about the contents of the box. The angel gave a simple and very somber response, "It contains all the blessings that God wanted to bestow upon you during your visit upon the earth, all the blessings that went unclaimed by you. The box contains what you could have had but chose to forgo by keeping your distance from God."

With that, the man backed away from the white chest. He knew all too well the truth of the angel's words. With tears in his eyes, they retreated from the great white building.

Conclusion

At the beginning of this book, I asked you to visualize what intimacy with God looks like in the life of a believer. What picture came to your mind? Was that picture attractive to you? Was it attainable? Is there a possibility that your picture may have included some false assumptions about intimacy with God? Is there any chance that you bought into a paradigm of the Christian life that has a clearly defined form and structure but is missing something at its core? Are you discouraged?

Authentic intimacy with God *is* available to you. It is something vital to your very identity. It is something powerful, something that continuously renews the excitement of your spiritual adventure, something that confirms the reality of your new life in Christ. The blessings in "the box" are real. God longs for you to enjoy them.

Come closer!

Drawing Closer

1. In what ways does your spiritual life resemble the work life of the senior flight attendant?

2. To which of the five distortions are you most susceptible? Why?

3. Which of the statements offered as a corrective to the five distortions is most appealing to you? Why?

4. Describe the last time you felt disappointment with God. What was the circumstance? How do you feel God failed you?

5. Put yourself into the "empty boxes" story. Well?

Part 2

The Passionate Pursuit

(So this is what it takes to be close to God!)

—⌒ FOUR ⌒—

Gazing into
the Eyes of God

(giving God access to your private life)

I HAVE NEVER HAD MUCH INTEREST IN SCIENCE. SO, WHEN IT CAME to fulfilling the general requirements for my bachelor's degree, I looked long and hard for the easiest possible solution in that category. It turned out that a neighboring college offered a course in astronomy that would satisfy the obligation. I enrolled.

The class was held in a theater-style auditorium that seated several hundred students. On the first day, I sized up the situation and made several observations. First, it was packed with students who had a "nonscience" look about them. Apparently, I wasn't the only one looking for a less technical alternative to science. Second, I learned that there would be no final exam. As long as I made an appearance at all the classes, I was guaranteed an A for the course. Third (and this is important) the auditorium filled from the back to the front. If you arrived early, you could have one of the choice seats high in the "nose-bleed" section. Otherwise, you could get stuck toward the front.

Near the end of the term, the professor carried out an annual ritual by surprising the class with an astronomy aptitude test. As the thick, multiple-guess questionnaire was distributed, the instructor assured us that this exercise had absolutely no bearing on our final grade. That was good to hear because as I read through the first few questions, I realized that this was a hopeless cause for me.

With nothing at stake, I decided to speed up the process. It seems that the first answer in most multiple-choice exams is *d*. It is usually followed by an *a* and then a couple of *c* s. So that was the system I put into action. I moved through the pages in record time, ignoring the questions and concentrating on the pattern of the hash marks. As you might expect, I finished a bit too quickly, so I decided to go back and "check" my answers. They sounded pretty good to me. By then a couple of others had turned in their tests. I followed suit and left.

I arrived late to the next lecture. True to form, the good seats in the back were taken, and the only available space was in the front row. As I fumbled with my books and tried not to look too conspicuous, the professor talked about the aptitude test from the previous week. "I have given this test to thousands of students," he droned, "but we have someone in this class who has achieved the third highest score of all the students I have taught."

I wasn't paying much attention up to that point, but his next question shot adrenaline through my veins, "Is Steve Korch here tonight?" I was instantly embarrassed and could feel the heat radiating from my face. I slowly raised my hand as far as my shoulder, and every eye converged on my highly visible location.

When the instructor spotted me seated right beneath his nose, his expressionless face suddenly came to life. "Please notice where this young man is seated," he proudly pointed out. "This proves a theory I have held for many years. The brightest students always sit in the front. The B students are right behind them. And so it goes right on up to you people in the back row."

I didn't have the heart to tell him what had really happened. Opting for the easy way out, I let him bask in his discovery. Fortunately, he never approached me about pursuing a career in astronomy.

Life through One's Own Eyes

Like the professor, we all live our lives based on a set of presuppositions. There are certain notions that we believe are true, and we go through life looking for evidence to validate them. If we look long enough and hard enough, we can find evidence to support anything we want to believe. The older we get, the more evidence we have gathered and the more convinced we have become that we are right.

The truth is, however, that apart from Christ, our lives are driven by disinformation, distorted concepts of who we are and of what life is all about. We decide what we are going to believe. What we choose determines how we live, and how we live reveals the beliefs we have chosen. Any failure and dysfunction in our lives can be traced directly to our belief system. I once heard that behind every self-defeating behavior in our lives is a lie that we are believing. I have found that to be true. The lies touch every point of our lives. They are lies about God, about ourselves, and about other people. They permeate our thoughts about the past and the future, about heaven and hell, and about the purpose of this life. The lies include misconceptions about what will make us happy and about our most essential needs. They are lies concocted by self-centered hearts — yours and mine. Although these concepts are distortions of reality, we will always be able to find something that appears to support them. Being predisposed to a certain line of thought, we can arrange virtually any set of facts or experiences to fit our beliefs.

A biblical example of this is found in John 12:27–29. As Jesus prayed about his impending death, God spoke from heaven to audibly confirm the presence of the Messiah. Everyone at the scene heard exactly the same thing. But while everyone was exposed to the same set of facts, they had differing conclusions. Some reasoned that an angel had spoken. Others figured that there was a more natural explanation, like thunder. The problem is that reason, operating alone, invariably misinterprets the evidence. It can't help but do so because it has been programmed with inaccurate presuppositions.

The Scriptures present faith as a moral issue rather than as an intellectual one. It is a matter of the heart. It is there in our own private worlds that we decide who we are and who we want to become. We choose which inner controls will govern our actions; we choose our priorities and passions. This is where we dream and imagine what the future holds. This is where we conceal our fears and failures. It is a neatly arranged world of make-believe where everything works the way we want it to, a world in which we call the shots and define the terms. This is what the Bible refers to as the inner person, the heart, the soul.

The inner person is the real you and me — intangible yet more real than the physical body that is seen in this life. This part of us relates to God, but until the Almighty is allowed into this realm of our lives, we can never become close. Now allowing God to invade this private space can be terrifying, for the possibility exists that all we have counted on, all we have built our lives upon, is wrong or defective or imaginary. British author Malcolm Muggeridge poses the crucial question, "Can you live on the basis of what you say you believe — no matter where you take those beliefs, no matter what they come up against?"[1]

As a believer, I am surprised how little of God's reality, biblical truth, is allowed to touch my inner life and shape the "me" that lives there. Very little is allowed to disturb the core of my being. It is safely protected by justifying my existing presuppositions, redefining new input, and denying whatever threatens the security of being right. Most of life's data simply bustles around the exterior.

I find it frighteningly convenient to intellectualize my "faith," to contain it within a manageable belief system of principles and concepts to which I have a mental agreement but no relational attachment. It is a complex set of concepts and principles, facts and factoids,[2] that I am continuously expanding and rearranging. Not everything within the set can be substantiated, and conflicting ideas often create a troublesome dissonance. I learn to live with what makes no sense while searching for evidence to support what I want to believe. After all, everyone needs something to believe in, a philosophy of life, even if it is illogical or even bizarre. Quoting again from Malcolm Muggeridge, "It is often supposed that when people stop believing in God they believe in nothing, but the situation is far more serious. The truth is that when they stop believing in God they believe in anything."[3]

In the book *Through the Looking Glass*, Alice is confronted with the absurdity of believing the impossible apart from any reason. Her response is simple:

> "I can't believe that!" said Alice.
> "Can't you?" the Queen said in a pitying tone. "Try again: draw a long breath, and shut your eyes."
> Alice laughed. "There's no use trying," she said, "one can't believe impossible things."

"I dare say you haven't much practice," said the Queen. "When I was your age, I always did it for half-an-hour a day. Why, sometimes I've believed as many as six impossible things before breakfast."[4]

As we endeavor to walk with Christ, we are continually confronted with new insights that demand an overhaul of our presuppositions. Apart from recalibrating our core concepts of life, we will never change our patterns of living. We will continue to play out the same self-centered actions and attitudes we pursued before meeting the Savior. Proverbs 23:7 says, "As he [a man] thinks within himself, so he is."

Life through God's Eyes

Jesus ordered his life around a different set of presuppositions than did those around him. The basic concepts that drove his life included the fact that God was overwhelmingly present and intimately involved in the details of life, that God was in control of events, that nothing was impossible for Yahweh, that God loved him intensely and ferociously, and that there was something bigger going on, much of which included things that were unseen or beyond one's ability to fathom.

Jesus breathed life into the concept of faith. His life was filled with excitement, expectation, and adventure. He was quick to recognize the Father's fingerprints on every activity of daily life. Faith put a confidence in the voice of Jesus that caused everyone and everything to listen. Jesus was never worried or alarmed. Even when gales blasted across the Sea of Tiberias or when angry mobs collected their stone weapons, Jesus' composure remained undisturbed. The information others had overlooked, discarded, or trivialized — that information calmed the wind and disarmed the crowds.

There was always something unusual, something out of the ordinary, happening in Jesus' life. Bread was multiplied, and water was turned to wine. People were healed, and lives were changed. With a simple command, children were raised from their deathbeds, and loved ones hobbled out of stone mausoleums. Around Jesus, one could expect the unexpected. Life was never monotonous or predictable in his presence.

Faith was not something Jesus switched on and off as needed. Faith was not reserved for special events or desperate circumstances. It was a way of life and the essence of his intimate relationship with the Father. Jesus ordered his entire life according to what was actually true. Thus, the life of Jesus stood out in stark contrast to those around him. Noticeably absent were those self-defeating quirks of misconceived human behavior. In their place were movements that made sense — that matched God's moral law.

The Password

Faith is a basic concept of Christianity. It is such a primary element that early Christians were actually called "believers." Faith is not simply wishful thinking or hoping for the best. It is not just a good feeling about something. Faith is not merely a religious form of optimism or positive thinking. It is not true that if we want something bad enough or long enough, we will get it. Faith is not acting on a hunch or working against common sense. Operating on the basis of faith does not mean that we turn off our brains and go into a mental free fall.

The Hebrew word for "believe," the one used to identify Abraham as the prototype of faith, has some muscle to it. It means to realize that something is true and to establish that "something" as a fact. It means to settle an issue in one's mind and begin to order one's life on the basis of that conclusion. The Bible describes faith in terms of being confident to the point of expectation and convinced to the point of action. Hebrews 11:1 puts it this way: "Now faith is the assurance of things hoped for, the conviction of things not seen."

Faith frees us from worry. Worry is only possible by taking God out of life's equations. If we do so, we are left to respond to life's possibilities in a manner that consumes us mentally, emotionally, and physically. It is by faith that we recognize God in the midst of our circumstances. It is our growing trust in God that carries us through the tough times. Worry is replaced by confidence, not in ourselves, but in God.

Faith expands our perspective, allowing us to see life in terms of a bigger picture. When someone lives in a small world, everything in it seems big. Faith keeps us from being driven by insignificant trivia. Somewhere along the way I heard that a preoccupation with the insignificant makes it impossible to bring priorities into perspective.

Faith activates spiritual power in our lives, giving us the ability to overcome personal and circumstantial obstacles. First John 5:4 identifies faith as the essential element that overcomes the world. The Scriptures constantly related power to faith. Remember that in a certain village Jesus could not do any miracles because there was a void of faith. Faith is the password that grants us access to the things we need most.

Eye Contact with God

Eye contact is a fascinating phenomenon. When we establish a visual connection with another person, something is activated inside us. It can suddenly spark a thrill of excitement or a flush of embarrassment. We may long to catch a person's gaze or desperately seek to avoid it. There is something intensely personal about eye contact, something that speaks directly to the soul. As God's eyes scan the faces of those who roam this earth, Yahweh is looking for those whose eyes are looking back toward heaven, those with whom the Spirit can make eye contact.

Some believe that faith is an innate element in our makeup over which we have little or no control; that is, either one has the ability to believe, or one doesn't. That certainly is not the biblical picture. In fact, God is very direct and deliberate in biblical statements about our personal responsibility to live by faith: "The righteous [i.e., those in a right relationship with God] will live by faith" (Galatians 3:11, NIV) and "Without faith it is impossible to please God" (Hebrews 11:6, NIV). Simply put, the Lover of our souls wants eye contact.

The process of cultivating a biblical faith involves three essential steps. They are discovering the truth, experiencing the truth, and assimilating the truth. The first two parts of the equation are very familiar to most evangelical believers, but the third piece — the most crucial one — is seldom addressed.

Discovering the Truth

Romans 10:17 tells us that faith develops in response to what God says. The believing itself is not the issue. It is *what* we believe that matters. So until we expose ourselves to the Scriptures, nothing of eternal consequence occurs. In his book *Love Your God with All Your Mind*, professor of philosophy J. P. Moreland writes, "Faith is a power or skill to act in accordance with the nature of the kingdom of God, a trust in what we have reason to believe is true. Understood in this way, we see that faith is built on reason. We should have good reasons for thinking that Christianity is true before we dedicate ourselves completely to it."[5]

Although it may sound a bit heretical, I believe we can do a disservice to believers by making our time in God's Word revolve around two specific items: a technical development of theology and a practical application of concepts for living. I believe it is numbing to our relationship with God to spend time in the Word and come away satisfied with information, having defined God better, but having come no closer to him; having defined life better, but missing the One who is life itself. Let me take a shot at saying this well. The main point of delving into the Scriptures is to know the God who wrote them. We have missed the point, then, if we come away without having heard God's voice. We have come short if we do not see this Awesome One emerging from those autobiographical pages. Theology has no point apart from knowing God, and practical concepts are meaningless apart from living ever closer to the Creator. We are called into the Word to find *God* and, in doing so, to grow in our trust of him.

My approach to Scripture does not diminish the importance of honest, accurate study of the Bible, but it does change how and why we go about that study. This approach does not take anything away from the need to apply the Scriptures to our personal lives, but it certainly changes how and why we do it. The great devotional writer Oswald Chambers once said, "Faith is not a conscious thing, it springs from a personal relationship and is the unconscious result of believing someone."[6] Faith involves acting on the basis of what we know about God. It is not the facts about Yahweh that matter as much as what we have been able to translate into relational realities, turning propositional truth into personal truth.

There is a concept in psychology known as interference or displacement. It is the idea that new data tends to interfere with, or displace, whatever is already in one's mind. Obviously, this can either work for or against a person. When it comes to changing the thoughts that drive one's life, displacement provides a tremendous advantage. The more of God's Word we put into our minds, the more our old thoughts will find interference or be moved out.

As we approach God's Word, we must come with a willingness to be shown that we have had faulty or defective thinking — that we have been wrong. We must be willing to be corrected and directed. Ask yourself,

Am I willing to change my thinking?

Experiencing the Truth

God is faithful, but apart from personally experiencing it, we can never know that for sure. In practical terms, we choose to move closer to God. We step into God's world and allow God into ours. It is at this point that we actually experience reality and interact with God on his terms.

Twenty years ago, someone gave me a greeting card that made some clever reference to faith. On the front of the card was a tiny mustard seed encased in a clear plastic bubble. The card is gone, but the seed and its plastic home remain. I have kept them as a reminder that faith was never intended to be isolated and protected. If faith is to grow, it must be deliberately planted in the soil of life. This conscious decision is the tangible link between what we know and what we do. As we do what God says, we discover the truth of what he says. It is only in the doing that we experience God's faithfulness in exciting ways that touch our lives. Second Peter 1:3–9 instructs us to take what we know to be true and connect it to the components of our lives — one piece at a time.

A friend of mine once told me, "Steve, people my age [take a guess] don't intend to change. We have decided what is true and

how life works. We have established certain patterns of living that
we do not want disturbed." Ask yourself,

Am I willing to change my patterns of living?

Assimilating the Truth

It is in the changing of our minds that we find ourselves agreeing
with God and seeing life as God does. We can share thoughts, enjoy
the same moments, laugh and cry over the same things. The biblical
term for this is "repentance." The literal meaning of the word is "a
change of mind." It is a resetting of presuppositions, an authentic
shifting of a paradigm.

As we make personal conclusions about God based upon the personal disclosures in God's own words, our trust in God can become
part of who we are rather than something unusual for us. Changing our presuppositions changes what we go looking for in this life.
Instead of searching for evidence to support our own ideas, we
watch for the proof that God has provided to back up his Word.
Ask yourself,

Am I willing to change my presuppositions?

Faith becomes a truly life-transforming factor as we settle in our
minds what is true. Psalm 112:7 spells this out by saying that the one
who takes God seriously and trusts in him,

does not fear bad news, nor live in dread of what may happen. For he is
settled in his mind that Jehovah will take care of him (TLB).

Faith is an issue of what we believe God *can* do. Is God really the
omnipotent ruler of the universe? Is God really able to do anything?
Is nothing impossible for him? What is God *willing* to do? Even if God
is unlimited in power, capable of anything, is he willing to act on our
behalf? What is God not willing to do? Where is the line? What do
we believe God actually *wants* to do? What are his desires for us?
What is God longing to provide for us by way of power, privilege,
and pleasure? Unless we come to conscious conclusions about what
God has said about himself as Creator and about us as his creation,
unless we take what God has said and done and settle in our minds

that it is true, we are doomed to repeat lesson after lesson in the same course.

Our Reflection in God's Eyes

As we draw close enough to peer into the eyes of God, we recognize the gaze of one who is completely trustworthy. But we also find something else — our own image reflected in those loving eyes. As ones who are growing in our trust, what do we see?

We See One Who Prays

Although faith is a very personal dynamic that occurs at the core of our being, it does have some very visible marks. James says faith cannot be hidden, that it is displayed in the outworking of daily life (James 2:14–26). Perhaps the most obvious of these marks is prayer. Prayer is a very tangible indicator of the presence of faith. Through this very simple act, we look away from ourselves to the Creator. But prayer, by itself, is not the real mark. Faith is identified by what is brought before God and by the acceptance of God's response to requests and petitions.

As a special gift, Ruthie and I were given a weekend in San Francisco at a very exclusive hotel. The gift also included dinner at one of the best restaurants in the city. When we arrived, we were ushered to our table and told that our dinner had been fully covered. The anonymous donor had left explicit instructions that we were to "order big." We could have anything on the menu. All we had to do was ask. God likewise challenges us to "order big," to ask in prayer for what only God can do.

A growing faith is marked by prayer that reaches increasingly further beyond our own abilities — dreaming God-sized dreams and experiencing God-sized responses. My father-in-law had a motto: When you live by faith, you have to take whatever God gives you, even if it is the best. Author Jerry Bridges writes, "By praying we recognize our helplessness and dependence. By praying we recognize that we are not in control of our lives, our health, our plans, or the decisions other people make respecting us."[7]

We See One Who Risks

Faith is unmistakable in the willingness to put oneself at risk. Authentic, biblical faith is always moving one outside zones of comfort. It is displayed in the courage to live differently from others.

As faith pervades our thinking, we don't find ourselves talking about what is safest or easiest or most comfortable. Initially, faith is experimental. We decide to take God at his word and venture into unknown territory. By faith, we choose to do what is unnatural for us.

With his insights and instructions for life, God provides enough evidence that the believing heart can have confidence but never so much as to eliminate the need for faith. Faith always has an unknown element to it. There is always a risk. There is always some question unanswered or some danger that remains a very real possibility. There is always something that cannot be foreseen or anticipated, something that cannot be controlled or manipulated. To live by such faith means that one forfeits the right to pass judgment on the wisdom God provides and chooses not to demand answers where God has chosen not to give them.

We See One Who Praises

Faith becomes audible in the praises of those who genuinely take God at his word and choose to trust Yahweh's heart. They boast about what God has done. They speak of God with a sense of awe and wonder. Their expectations of the Mighty One are always increasing. It is displayed in the depth and richness of their worship. There is life in it.

Conclusion

Learning to trust our Savior-Prince and follow him is a process. This short story by Pat Westfall helps to portray what that process is.

> Once there was a princess who lived imprisoned in a tower high above the clouds.
>
> One day a great prince heard her plea for help, rescued her from the tower and brought her down to earth.
>
> There her heart filled as he declared his love for her. She gratefully accepted his offer to guide and protect her on the journey to his palace.

As they traveled he showed her some of the rich bounty of the earth he hoped they could share together.

But she found she didn't like the earth. It was strange to her feet. It had ruts, bumps, rocks and humps so she often tripped and fell, bruising her knees, scraping her hands, or even hitting her head on the ground.

All of this made her so angry she would stamp her feet and scream at the patient prince. She would pace back and forth, mostly back, her arms crossed defiantly in front of her, muttering how unfair it was for princesses to have to walk on such bad roads.

In her heart she cursed the prince for taking her from her high tower. This wasn't what she had expected at all. If he cared about her why didn't he do something instead of making her feel all alone in the heat and dirt?

Sometimes people would pass by and stare rudely at her dusty face or smirk at her muddy white dress. Then she would remember her cool quiet tower where she had looked down from the window at the people on the road below, so tiny that they looked like colored marbles rolling through a maze.

How she yearned for those days. How she wished she could return to her tower.

Well, one day her wish was granted. She saw a side road with a sign pointing back to her tower and decided to follow it. The way back seemed much shorter than the way she had come. Eagerly she ran up the stairs and into her old room, closing the door behind her.

And what did she find there? Leaks in the roof. Cracked walls that chilled her feet. Even the view from her window made her sick to her stomach.

She had grown used to sky and trees and rolling hills forever in front of her. The princess longed to feel the soft dust beneath her feet, the prickly grass, and cool wet puddles after the rain. She wanted the freedom of dragging her white dress behind her in the rutted road. She missed seeing people's faces close up. Most of all she found she missed the prince.

She beat her fists against the close encircling walls and wept.

One day, full of longing to be free again, she tried the door, fully expecting it to be locked. It opened wide.

There on the other side, faithfully waiting for her, was her wonderful prince.

Her heart and feet both leaped as he held out his arms to her. Together they walked down the stairs and out onto the road, leaving the tower to crumble slowly behind them.

Once again she walks along the bumpy road, still falling occasionally but rising to walk on. Sometimes she stops to help others who have fallen.

Her eyes now follow the prince who still walks just a little ahead of her, while over a high mountain the gates to his palace are opening.[8]

We must be willing to change our presuppositions and order our lives around God's statements of reality. We must be willing to see life through God's eyes by gazing into those eyes.

Drawing Closer

1. Apart from yourself, whom do you depend on most in this life? In what ways do you depend on that person? How is that dependence similar to faith in God?

2. In what specific circumstances are you currently finding yourself totally dependent upon God? In what ways are you dependent?

3. What is one issue in your life that you do not see eye to eye with God? Why do you think there is a difference in your thinking?

4. What is your greatest fear about giving God access to your inner life? What will it take to overcome that fear?

5. In what ways do you see yourself in the princess?

___୧ FIVE ୨___

Dancing in the Arms of God

(nurturing an authentic passion for God)

W E SAT FOUR ROWS BACK IN AN AUDITORIUM FILLED TO CAPACITY. It was a special evening — Good Friday. The stage was sparsely set. Black curtains adorned the curved walls. The main feature was a large cross off to one side, dimly lit with a single spotlight.

As the worship service got underway, I noticed a young woman enter and take a seat in the front row. She wore a plain, long black dress that covered her arms and buttoned up to her throat. Her head was covered with a white scarf that was wrapped once beneath her chin and thrown back over her shoulders. The scarf framed the Palestinian features of this woman's face.

The service progressed through its well-crafted movements, the last of which was an extended time of praise music. We prayed before singing, and when I opened my eyes, I found that my lady in black was on the stage kneeling at the foot of the cross. Then as we lifted our voices in song, the woman rose to her feet and began to dance lightly across the platform. Her graceful movements matched the music and added a visible dimension to the words we sang.

The woman's long black dress covered white billowing pants that were gathered at the ankles, just above her dancing slippers. The dark velvet of the outer garment absorbed the light and conveyed a somber feeling of mourning. But when she whirled about, the brilliant white of the flowing layers appeared and shouted her joy. Her sheer white scarf followed her movements, leaving a wisp of an outline

65

in the air. The music quickened, and the dancer leapt and twirled with a passion that came from somewhere deep within her being. It was obvious that she was thoroughly enjoying the freedom of her worship. This was no performance; it was more like a private affair that we were privileged to witness. Perhaps it was much like the angels watching each of us in our personal encounters with God.

At some point in the midst of the experience, I realized why the dancing was making such an impact upon me. As words formed in my mind, I almost spoke them audibly. That's my own spirit dancing with my Lord, I thought to myself. She is doing up there what my spirit is doing within me — dancing in the arms of God.

Onto the Dance Floor

Worship is the central word in the love story told throughout the pages of the Bible. God's people are pictured collectively as a beautiful bride who worships her loving Prince. She adores everything about him. She longs to be in his presence and to hear his voice. She pores over his love letters, absorbing every detail of his life and of what he has done for her. She is in awe of a love so immense that she cannot stifle it with her failures. She is overwhelmed that he would choose her as the object of such love. She cherishes their intimacy and revels in the purity of their love. She would gladly do anything for him without the slightest feeling of imposition. Somehow she seems to bring him up in every conversation, making others envious of what she has found in him. The very thought of the Prince draws music from the core of her being, and she anxiously awaits the next opportunity to dance in his arms.

A Daily Encounter

God longs for us to walk into each day with a renewed love for him, one that sets our spirit dancing. It is our love for God that is to drive how we live, and it is our worship of God that fuels such love. In other words, if we are not intentionally setting aside time to worship each day, we cannot expect to deepen our love for God. If our love for God is not continually growing, our life as a Christian will tend to become more of a mechanical obligation rather than a natural expression of intimacy with God. Therefore, it is vital to our spiritual health that we dedicate time each day for the specific purpose of drawing close to God. It is not just a time for gaining biblical information or updating our list of things for God to do. It must be a time of personal encounter with him, a time for standing on holy ground — without sandals.

Personal worship is vital because it is at the heart of how we relate to God. It is the driving passion of our relationship with God, the very essence of intimacy. Worship is to be a consuming pattern of our lives, highlighted by moments of concentrated adoration. There is nothing casual about it. Pastor and author John McArthur describes worship as a lifestyle: "It involves all that we are, reacting to all that God is."[1] As such, worship is the act of being caught up in the wonder of this Awesome One. It is giving God our full, undivided attention, not as a spiritual discipline, but in an effort to move closer to God, to discover something new about him, or to clarify the reality of God's presence. William Temple, the archbishop of Canterbury, observed that worship is "to quicken the conscience by the holiness of God, to feed the mind with the truth of God, to purge the imagination by the beauty of God, to open the heart to the love of God, and to devote the will to the purpose of God."

As we worship, we direct our hearts toward God and intentionally deepen our love for him. Each time we do so, we are choosing to love God. We are deciding once again to throw ourselves into God's arms. The decision is driven, not by how we feel, but by what we know to be true. Author Eugene Peterson rightly observes,

> We think that if we don't feel something there can be no authenticity in doing it. But the wisdom of God says something different, namely, that we can act ourselves into a new way of feeling much quicker than we can feel ourselves into a new way of acting. Worship is an act which develops feelings for God, not a feeling for God which is expressed in an act of worship. When we obey the command to praise God in worship, our deep, essential need to be in relationship with God is nurtured.[2]

For worship to become an intimate expression of the heart, the heart must first be moved and then given the freedom to dance. We do so by first directing our attention to the beauty of God's person and to the intense love God has for us. This requires time in the

Scriptures, absorbing this truth. While the act of worship focuses our attention upon God in such a way as to nurture our love for him, it also provides the opportunity for us to express the love that has been cultivated in our heart. Writing about this aspect of worship, Oswald Sanders says, "Worship flows from love. Where love is meager, worship will be scant. Where love is deep, worship will overflow."[3]

It is in the process of worship that we make several discoveries. Early on, we discover that worship is not enough. We learn that worship, as Eugene Peterson says, "does not satisfy our hunger for God — it whets our appetite. Our need for God is not taken care of by engaging in worship — it deepens."[4]

We also discover the profound effect such personal encounters have upon us. Johann Wolfgang von Goethe (a German poet born in the eighteenth century) once made the comment, "We are fashioned and shaped by what we love." If that is true, then the deeper our love for God grows, and the longer that love is nurtured, the more we will become like the One we are loving. Our lives will be changed by this love relationship with God. In his book *The Celebration of Discipline*, Richard Foster writes, "If worship does not change us, it has not been worship. To stand before the Holy One of eternity is to change.... In worship an increased power steals its way into the heart sanctuary, an increased compassion grows in the soul. To worship is to change."[5]

Another discovery is in the realm of our self-image. Worshiping God keeps us from worshiping ourselves. We are in continual need of being reminded of who God is and of who God is not. Consider the story of the French king Louis XIV:

> In 1717, Louis XIV of France died. Louis who called himself "the Great," was the monarch who declared, "I am the State!" His court was the most magnificent in Europe and his funeral the most spectacular. His body lay in a golden coffin. To dramatize his greatness, orders had been given that the cathedral would be very dimly lighted with only a special candle set above the coffin. Thousands waited in hushed silence. Then Bishop Massilon began to speak. Slowly reaching down, he snuffed out the candle, saying, "only God is great."[6]

We need to hear that each day.

When we come honestly before the throne of God, we are forced to fall on our knees and acknowledge his greatness. We find ourselves face-to-face with God, lost in the wonder of our relationship. Michael Wiebe has pointed out that "worship is our primary response to God's essential majesty."[7]

Finally, we discover that worshiping God is what we are really all about. We are most true to who we are when we are involved in worship. To be fully focused upon God, singing love songs, shouting praises, and visibly displaying the pleasure of Yahweh's presence, quietly leaning into him and relishing the sound of God's words from the pages of his letter — this is what we were created for. It is such encounters with God that bring perspective to our lives. Worship helps us sort out what really matters. Timothy Christenson expressed that reality with these words: "If worship is just one thing we do, everything becomes mundane. If worship is *the* one thing we do, everything takes on eternal significance."

I like the way Elizabeth Barrett Browning puts it.

> Earth's crammed with heaven,
> And every common bush afire with God:
> But only he who sees, takes off his shoes,
> The rest sit round it, and pluck blackberries.[8]

An Intimate Event

While worship is personal, it is not exclusively private. Worship requires our personal response to God, but there are times when we are to bring this response as part of something bigger.[9] Gathering with other believers for worship should be the main attraction of the week, not as a social event, but as a powerful extension of personal worship. On a corporate level, worship is the collective adoration of God by those he has redeemed. It is the church, as one body, that is the bride of Christ. It is to this complex bride, rather than to individuals, that virtually all of the New Testament instruction is given concerning worship.

Theologian Karl Barth described worship as "the most momentous, the most urgent, the most glorious action that can take place in human life." It should be something we look forward to with great anticipation. It should be something that we prepare for, knowing that God has looked forward to that gathering from eternity past and has personal intentions for that event. Also, it should be something that leaves its mark upon our soul as we proceed into the week. It might be good for us to order our week according to the Tonganese calendar. In Tonga, worship is actually built into the names given to the days of the week. Saturday means "prepare for worship," Sunday means "day of worship," and Monday means (as you might expect) "the day after worship."

For too many of God's people, glorious and momentous worship is not the case. It may be that something is not right in the spiritual lives of such people. Or it may be that the public worship gatherings they attend have drifted into a lifeless predictability. Personally, I believe it is dangerous to our spiritual health to have services formatted to be familiar, comfortable, and safe. When church bulletins can be recycled week after week by simply changing a few names and numbers, we are in trouble. Believers begin to develop a robotic routine, knowing just when to stand up and sit down, when to open a hymnal, and when to pull out a billfold. In many churches, one could actually sleep through a service and never really miss anything of eternal consequence; some do (sleep, that is).

For several years, I had this concept driven home each week in a small church I pastored straight out of seminary. We met in a tiny building at the end of an unmarked street. The little box held a maximum of seventy-five people. Creaking wood furniture, rustling paper, and private comments were all amplified within the cozy space. It provided a wonderful environment for singing but added considerable background noise to the quieter portions of our worship. There was one older gentleman in our midst who had difficulty hearing and would consistently doze off within a few minutes after the service got underway. That wasn't so bad. We all understood the situation. However, things would become a bit more problematic when he would begin a loud rasping snore that reverberated off the walls. While stifling my laughter, I often wondered how many other souls were asleep in worship services — with their eyes wide open.

Seeing people conk off in a worship service is a signal that something is dreadfully wrong. Are believers snoozing through their Sunday mornings because they cannot hear the sounds of the service or because they cannot hear the music from heaven? Is something missing in the very design of our worship? I am convinced that boring services are foreign to the biblical concept of worship and offensive to God. In such events, the minds of would-be worshipers are allowed to traipse off into the trivia of life. If God's people are not ushered into the presence of their God, it is easy to understand why they might begin looking for something to bring some pizzazz to a stale experience. For such people, Tim Sims and Dan Pegoda come to the rescue with a humorous collection of things to do in the doldrums of a dull service. Sims and Pegoda suggest seeing how many words you can make from the name "Methuselah," trying to crawl under the pews from the back of the church to the front, blowing bubbles, and shouting misplaced "amen"s.[10] Of course, there is a far better option — learn to dance.

Samaritan Dance Lesson

While traveling through the region of Samaria, Jesus had a conversation with a local woman. The exchange that took place with this woman was no surface conversation. It was an intimate interaction between a searching dancer and the God of the music.

The people in that area had developed an alternative to the mainline worship centered in Jerusalem. It drew from history and from local traditions. Their worship included elements of truth mixed with secular philosophies. It seemed to provide some common ground in a multicultural community, but the focus was really on the people themselves, rather than on God. It was their personal preferences that provided the framework for their form of worship. What they got out of a service was more important than what God got out of it. (Sound familiar?) I don't imagine that their services were boring, but they were far too earthy and incapable of bringing people together with the true God. While the Samaritan woman attempted to defend her homemade version of worship, Jesus helped her place the main feature back in place.

You see, when authentic, everything in worship takes attention off of us and places it on God. True worship involves singing about God. It is bringing sacrifices and offerings — gifts to him. Worship includes God's Word (listening to him) and prayer (talking to him).

It is praising and thanking and asking forgiveness from God. Seminary professors Ronald Allen and Gordon Borror emphasize all this in their book on worship: "Worship is about God, not man. The worship of God does do many things for us as individuals and as a community. But true worship should be defined in terms of God first of all. Worship is about God, and worship is what God desires from us."[11] As we learn from the Gospel of John, "The true worshipers shall worship the Father in spirit and truth; for such people the Father seeks to be His worshipers" (John 4:23).

Dance Step 1: Worship in Spirit

While speaking to the Samaritan woman, Jesus pointed out that the primary issue is not the location of the services or the structure in which people meet. It is not the time of the event or the order of its components. Worship is not defined by such patterns or confined to such boundaries. True worship, Jesus said, is "in spirit."

On a tour of Jerusalem, I found myself standing on the temple mount. I tried to visualize what it must have been like two thousand years ago with the majestic structure as the focal point. Biblical scholars, historians, and archaeologists have merged their insights into conclusions and have suggested the exact location and positioning of the temple on this high ground of Jerusalem. If they are right, it is possible to actually stand on the site of the very Holy of Holies — the sacred heart of the temple. I did that. I stood there for a moment and tried to imagine what it would have been like to step behind the curtain and into God's presence. Then I reminded myself that in the New Testament our bodies are referred to as the temple of God. We are what you might call a "mobile worship unit." We are completely equipped for worship at any time and in any place. God has set up personal residence within us. God's Holy of Holies is now in my heart and in yours.

A certain freedom comes from knowing that our worship of God is not shackled to any particular time or space. We are not restricted to a one-hour time slot on Sunday morning. We don't have to come within the walls of a specific structure, outfitted with pews and stained-glass windows. We don't have to dress a certain way or go through certain motions. There are no tangible objects or visible procedures associated with worship that is "in spirit."

Worship in spirit not only deemphasizes the physical; it throws the emphasis to the relational. True worship involves our spirit relating to God's Spirit. It involves developing a sense of God's presence in our lifestyle. To worship in spirit is to emphasize this relational aspect. Just as dancing is moving with a person, so worship is moving with God. Dancing requires that we hear the same music and move to the same rhythm. It is a matter, not of moving as one person with identical actions, but of moving in such a manner as to complement the movements of the other person and reveal an awareness and a responsiveness to each other.

Dance Step 2: Worship in Truth

Worshiping in truth involves worshiping the true God and doing so with authenticity. It is impossible to worship *in* truth apart from *the* truth of God's Word. It is not bitter truth that comes with a rule book and manacles, but truth that tastes like honey and sets us free. It is truth that illuminates our dark world and provides the musical score for the timbre of eternity. I have heard it said that hope is hearing the music from a distant land and that faith is dancing to that music.

In order to worship the true God, we must clear away our self-designed image of him, misconceptions we have fostered in an effort to have God fit into our plan for this life. We must discard the rumors we have heard about what God is like and about how God deals with us. Worship in truth is a matter of coming ever closer to the Creator and seeing God for who he really is. To accomplish this, we must approach the Scriptures relationally. As we study God's Word, our primary goal must be to *know* God. As we pore over the words, we must search out God's mind and heart and purposes. We must look for what makes God laugh and what breaks God's heart. It is a spiritual exercise that first brings us to our knees and then lifts us into Yahweh's arms. David Needham writes, "In every circumstance when a believer allows himself to be confronted with his God, he will worship. God, rightly perceived, will always be a God too big."[12]

Worshiping in truth not only involves worshiping the true God but also means worshiping authentically. Again, the Scriptures provide the only basis for such worship. It is there that we discover how to pray and praise, how to listen to God's voice, how to respond as an individual and as part of a group, how to be quiet before God, and how to dance in his arms.

A sense of wonder about God is embedded in the very nature of worship. British writer and editor G. K. Chesterton closed in on the need within us to be in the presence of something bigger than ourselves. He wrote, "We will never starve for the want of wonders, but only for the want of wonder." William Quayle adds the consequence of such a vacuum. "When wonder is dead," he wrote, "the soul becomes a dry bone."

Moving with the Music

In recent years, most of the weddings I have been involved with have been followed by lavish receptions and dancing. It is fun to watch what happens when "church people" step onto the dance floor. It is almost as though becoming a believer disables the creative motion signals from the brain to the feet — and everything in between. I envy those who seem to have a natural sense of movement and who can translate music into bodily motion.

Learning to worship is like learning to dance. We begin by learning specific steps like praise and prayer, communion with God and communion with other believers. There are certain mechanics of worship drawn from God's Word that guide the placement of our feet. In order to carry out this analogy and present myself as somewhat of an authority, I picked up some books from the library on dancing. For example, I checked out a no-nonsense volume entitled *The Complete Book of Ballroom Dancing*. Now, that sounds like all any slightly coordinated and reasonably motivated dancing recruit would need. The book includes detailed instructions for everything from the waltz and the fox-trot to the rumba and the tango and even the polka. There were black-and-white photographs of couples posing in various dance positions and shoe-print diagrams with numbers, arrows, and dotted lines to plot the progression of the dance. The man's part and the woman's part were shown. There was more than enough information about dancing. But simply knowing what to do did not mean that I could actually make it happen on the dance floor. It takes practice!

Another book I picked up was written by Teri Loren. She offered this advice:

> There's a great deal of detail in dancing — many different parts of your body to move, directions to move them in, dynamics to use, rhythms to follow, phrases to recognize. When you're just beginning, all these details can present a staggering amount to learn. It's important to remember, though, that dancing is movement, and not just details about movement. As a beginner, try not to worry so much about performing every last minute item absolutely correctly. Instead, try to build your sense of movement.[13]

I like that idea as it relates to worship — trying to build a sense of movement.

A word of encouragement came from one of my daughters who loves to dance. She said that the best dancers are not necessarily those with the best moves but those who look like they are having fun. It was similar to what dancing expert Margaret H'Doubler once said, "Good dancing is not concerned with a beautiful body moving, but rather with a body moving beautifully."[14]

It has been said that dancing is an integral part of life itself.[15] I love to dance (although I am slightly challenged in this area). There are times when the emotions of my heart search for an expression that captures my entire being, one that allows the inner person to emerge in some tangible form. There are times when my spirit dances in ways my physical body cannot begin to replicate. With that in mind, I have contemplated enrolling in classes to learn various dance steps — waltz, swing, line dance.

Teri Loren offered some additional encouragement:

> "Mental practice" is defined as performing a physical activity in your head without using your body... when you imagine a movement, you actually send "action currents" or slight nervous impulses to the muscles that are supposed to be used during the movement. Although these impulses remain beneath the conscious level and don't actually move any muscles, they are rehearsed subconsciously by your nervous system, so that when you next try the skill, the right impulses are there to be called upon.[16]

This makes me think of preparing for worship. Thinking ahead about dancing in the arms of God sets us up for the kind of experience that the Creator intended in worship. We can anticipate both the thrill of Yahweh's presence as well as the calming effect of being so close to God.

Worship Thrills the Heart

The very fact of being in someone's presence can be a thrill, even if no words are exchanged. In 1976, I was attending seminary in Portland, Oregon. That was the year President Gerald Ford came to town and decided to attend a service at the same church where Ruthie and I worshiped. It turned out to be a fascinating morning. A frustrated security team attempted to check the note-crammed Bibles for bombs, as worshipers streamed by. As it turned out, we sat only a half dozen rows in front of the president, and just enough to one side that we didn't have to turn completely around to gawk at him.

I can remember the excitement of being that close to one of the most powerful people on earth. And yet I was actually sitting closer to the most powerful Presence in the universe. While the president didn't even know I existed, God was intently interested in me and desired the intimacy of the experience to be an emotional charge for me.

Worship Stills the Heart

In the presence of God, our fears are calmed. The same attributes of God that cause us to fall down before him also bring a sense of safety and security. The intimate prayer of Scottish minister and hymn writer George Matheson conveys the quiet heart of one who is drawing close to Yahweh:

O Thou divine Spirit that, in all events of life, art knocking at the door of my heart, help me to respond to Thee. I would not be driven blindly as the stars over their courses. I would not be made to work out Thy will unwillingly, to fulfill thy law unintelligently, to obey Thy mandates unsympathetically. I would take the events of my life as good and perfect gifts from Thee; I would receive even the sorrows of life as disguised gifts from Thee. I would have my heart open at all times to receive — at morning, noon, and night; in spring and summer and winter. Whether Thou comest to me in sunshine or in rain, I would take Thee into my heart joyfully. Thou art Thyself more than the sunshine, Thou art Thyself compensation for the rain; it is Thee and not Thy gifts I crave; knock, and I shall open unto Thee. Amen.

Conclusion

David was dancing before the LORD with all his might...leaping and dancing before the LORD. (2 Samuel 6:14–16)

The very idea of coming into the presence of God should cause such a delight to one's heart that it leaps with joy and dances before him. Each heart longs to take hold of Christ's nail-scarred hand in Communion, to hear the music of heaven in the praises of God's people, to listen to the whispers of God's voice as his Word is spoken, to carry the conversation back to God in prayer, and to do it all while myriads of angels watch each of us alone with the Lord of the universe...dancing.

Drawing Closer

1. Browse through the chapter and review the quotations about worship. Which of these stands out most in your mind? Why?

2. Would you describe your worship of God as "intimate"? Why or why not?

3. In very specific terms, how do you believe your personal worship of God affects your corporate worship? How does your corporate worship affect your personal worship?

4. What do you do to prepare for corporate worship? What do you believe you *should* do to prepare?

5. Design what you believe would be an "ideal" format for personal worship. How long would it be? What would be done? Where? When?

─᷍ SIX ᷍─

Delighting in the Mind of God

(hearing God's voice with your whole being)

S OME OF MY MOST CHERISHED CHILDHOOD MEMORIES TAKE ME BACK to a two-story farmhouse in Illinois, complete with a treasure-filled attic and a dark, spooky basement. For a few brief weeks each summer, I spent my days playing with the kids from a neighboring farm. The warm nights were devoted to chasing fireflies around the acres of lawn that wrapped around the old house. It was the home of my grandparents.

During those summer breaks, one of the great joys was to have my grandfather to myself. I can remember a few very special times when he would take me on an adventure. We would climb through the split-rail fence into a wheat field. With my hand firmly grasped, he would lead me through the sea of stalks. I couldn't see where we were going since the field had grown taller than I. The path ahead would open before us as my grandfather took his steps.

Our destination was a grove of trees about a hundred yards away, a place we called "the woods." It was there that my grandfather would tell me the most fascinating stories, tales that played with my imagination. As I listened, I discovered that there was an entire world of unseen creatures living just beyond my sight. Tiny elves and winged fairies were everywhere. I never doubted that they were there. My grandfather was always able to find evidence of their presence: hidden trails, secret dwellings, and the faint sound of voices in the breeze. I think I might have actually seen a few of them and may have unknowingly crushed a home or two while searching.[1]

My grandfather also told stories about the very visible world I lived in, about the plants and animals that surrounded us. We would listen to the birds calling to each other, and he would help me distinguish between a martin and a finch. We would find bugs and beetles and odd little creatures that delight a child's heart. He would point out colors and shapes and shafts of light. That small forest was a magical place when my grandfather was in it.

The stories included chronicles of my grandfather's own history. They were adventures that occurred long before I existed. He had been a soldier in the army and a cowboy with a horse and real gun. He had built a log cabin in the mountains of Montana and had personally fought with "bad guys." What a hero!

Grandfather may have told those stories (or at least some of them) to a thousand other people over the years, but in those warm summer moments they were private stories meant only for me. His words brought me inside his mind and allowed me to look at the world with a sense of wonder. With him I could practice looking beyond what I could actually see and touch. The resonance of his voice was more than just another sound in the woods. It captured my entire being. It changed who I am and how I think.

Wondrous Words

The law of the LORD is perfect, restoring the soul;
The testimony of the LORD is sure, making wise the simple.
The precepts of the LORD are right, rejoicing the heart;
The commandment of the LORD is pure, enlightening the eyes.
The fear of the LORD is clean, enduring forever;
The judgments of the LORD are true; they are righteous altogether.
They are more desirable that gold, yes, than much fine gold;
Sweeter also than honey and the drippings of the honeycomb.
Moreover, by them Thy servant is warned;
In keeping them there is great reward.

— Psalm 19:7–11

The Wonder of Who Is Speaking

When I met with my grandfather in the shade of that island grove, it was not for the purpose of recording his words or pondering the depths of his insights. He did not have me bring a pencil and notepad in order to jot down pertinent truth that I would need later in life. Hey, I was just a little boy hanging out with his grandpa. The conversation was intended to be relational more than instructional.

Today, I can't remember the details of his stories, but I will never forget the experience of sitting with him in that mystical woodland. I can vividly recapture the sound of his voice, the smell of his cologne, and the gentle expression on his face. It was the wonder of *who* was speaking that was most significant. That is what has marked my mind and heart forever.

Could it be that we miss the wonder of what God says because we miss the wonder of who is saying it? Could it be that God longs to have the same type of experience with us that I had with my grandfather? After all, what's the point of God's communicating with us? Isn't it all about knowing God and enjoying him forever? Pastor and author A. W. Tozer once wrote, "God is so vastly wonderful, so utterly and completely delightful, that he can without anything other than himself meet and overflow the deepest demands of our total nature, mysterious and deep as that nature is."[2] That is the wonder of *who* is speaking.

The Wonder of What Is Said

As God speaks to us, we are ushered inside Yahweh's mind and exposed to a completely different way of thinking and of seeing the world around us. The wonder of this is expressed by the apostle Paul:

> "No eye has seen, no ear has heard, no mind has conceived what God has prepared for those who love him" — but God has revealed it to us. (1 Corinthians 2:9–10, NIV)

God tells us about what lies just beyond our senses. He describes breathtaking scenes of vast gardens and lavish palaces and tells true-life stories about terrifying spirit creatures waging war all around us. God explains how this world came into being and how it came into its present condition. Yahweh* walks us through the blueprints of our personal design and shows us how to live a life that is meaningful and purposeful. God reveals the secrets of how life works and helps us make sense out of the jumbled events of history. Taking us behind

*Refer to Chapter One. This is God's personal name.

the scenes, he reveals human hearts and a divine master plan. God tells us stories of those who have trusted him and found him faithful to his promises and also recounts the lives of some who have defied the Creator and found him faithful to the warnings.

Wonderful truth. In speaking, God not only presents to us a completely different way of thinking, but God also exposes the wonderful truth about who we are in relation to him. Hearing the truth has the wonderful power to recast our image and bring us back to reality.

On January 26, 1997, at the age of forty-six, my identity was changed. One of the most basic questions I could be asked would receive a different answer from that day forward. To understand this, you must know something about my past. Shortly after I was born, my parents divorced. My father, being a citizen of Sweden, returned to his Scandian home and was no longer a part of my life. My mother then remarried and had two more children — my brother and sister. This is the family I grew up with.

I can honestly say that I never really put any thought into what had become of my father. I suppose I could be charged with a deplorable lack of curiosity. I don't recall any conversations about him. There were no photos of him and no letters from Sweden. Apart from my last name, which had never been changed, there was no evidence that Bengt Eric Korch had ever existed.

A few years ago, my wife began searching for the missing pieces of my life. Because I showed no interest in this genealogical endeavor, she investigated on her own. It was a frustrating experience for her, filled with many dead-end streets. To expand her resources, she involved our teenage son — our computer ace. He ran a name search on the Internet and found some Korch addresses in Sweden. He chose one and sent a message asking for help in the quest.

It was on January 26, 1997, that Ruthie and Travers presented me with the e-mailed response: "Yes, I do know of a Bengt Korch." The message included other information about the Scandinavian side of my family. I discovered that my father had died precisely one year earlier. I also learned that I had two brothers and two sisters that I had never known existed.

I spent the next few weeks absorbing the reality of this information and sorting out what it all meant. I was no longer a person with one brother and one sister. Now I had three of each. There were new in-laws, nieces, and nephews. In a moment's time, with one short message from Sweden, my identity had changed. The circumstances of life remained the same, but who I was in the midst of them was now different. The facts, the realities of my life, had always been there. I had just been unaware of them. These people did not just suddenly appear when I discovered them. My relationship to them was not made any more valid by this information, but it was in hearing the facts and believing them that my life was altered in practical terms.

In the months that followed, there were many letters, e-mails, and telephone conversations. Gifts and photographs were exchanged. There were endless questions and fascinating answers. It has been a fun time of discovering a whole new world. It has amazed me just how much this new information has changed life for me.

In a similar manner, God brings us new information about who we are in relation to him. God's written Word documents our past and reveals our true identity. It supplies the missing pieces and answers questions we haven't even dared to ask. As God speaks, he calls us to come close — where we were meant to be. Because of hearing spiritual truth, we see God differently, we see ourselves differently, and we respond to the most basic questions of life with different answers. This, too, is the wonder of *what* is being said.

Although the truth of God's Word is there all along, our aware-ness of such realities may not come until we have traveled through many years of life. We may have no interest in discovering it, being content with whatever fragments of information we have possessed. Even though we may have known more was out there somewhere, an encounter with such information can have a transforming effect.

Learning to Listen

Frank Buchman once challenged believers with these words, "When man listens, God speaks. When man obeys, God acts. . . . We are not out to tell God. We are out to let God tell us. . . . The lesson the world most needs is the art of listening to God."[3] He was right. But how does one actually develop the art of listening to God?

By Fully Indulging in God's Word

God invites us to fully indulge the craving within us for spiritual substance. Apart from this feast, there is no possibility of spiritual growth. This is not a matter of sampling tidbits of truth or savoring morsels of insight. It is not an exercise in tinkering with terms or cultivating a selective diet of particularly appealing concepts. It is feasting as a famished peasant. It is responding to the insatiable hunger within by consuming all that is placed before us:

> Like newborn babes, long for the pure milk of the word, that by it you may grow in respect to salvation. (1 Peter 2:2)

Bonsai Christians. Bonsai trees are miniature replicas of full-grown trees that have been beautifully manipulated with an artistic eye. By nature, these trees should reach a stature of ten to twenty feet. They should have stout trunks and hefty branches that spread over a wide radius. So how is their pygmy status achieved? There are two basic procedures involved. First, the taproot is tied off when the sapling first sprouts. The primary source of nourishment for the tree is restricted so that no matter how much is provided, the fledgling arbor can draw only enough to survive. Second, evidences of new growth are selectively cut off as soon as they appear. In this way, growth is controlled, and the tree takes whatever form the artisan chooses.

It is possible to live as "Bonsai" Christians, restricting the intake of spiritual sustenance, although surrounded by the rich teaching of God's Word. By limiting what we absorb and by refusing to allow natural growth to occur when and where God produces it, we end up manipulating the Christian life into a dwarfed caricature of what God intended.

If we are only hearing what we want to hear, then it is most likely true that we are not really listening at all. We are merely flagging smidgens of truth that happen to catch our attention because of their familiarity with what we already believe. Consequently, nothing changes: not us, not our relationships with God, nothing. But by allowing the fullest measure of God's Word to invade our soul, what God says can permeate our entire being. His words can affect every aspect of our lives. With that infusion of truth, genuine changes begin to occur.

Part of what inhibits the indulgence of spiritual insight is the perception we attach to what we are being offered. If we perceive what God is saying as boring or irrelevant to our circumstances in life, we will tend to stop listening. We can become impatient and want to get on to the "good stuff." If we consider the exposure to God's Word to be primarily an academic exercise in a theological subject, we will probably start dozing off before God has the chance to speak.

A private window. Some of my most valuable documents are stored in an old shoe box. They are old love letters from the days when Ruthie and I were engaged but living hundreds of miles apart. Much of what is contained in those letters is simply history: a record of what Ruthie was doing on a certain day, what she enjoyed, what she thought about. If read for their historical value, they would be accurate — but boring and trivial. But when read as a window into a girl's heart, they are fascinating and deeply personal. In a similar way, God's Word is a window into the heart of a person. God gives us glimpses into his activities, along with the thoughts and emotions behind them. Recognizing the Scriptures as personal correspondence to us transforms the study of God's Word from an academic exercise to a personal adventure.

By Taking God Seriously

Philosopher and theologian Francis Schaeffer wrote, "The basis for our faith is that certain things are true. The whole man, including the intellect, is to act upon the fact that certain things are true. That, of course, will lead to an experiential relationship with God."[4] Choosing to face the truth of God's Word seriously and honestly puts us on the threshold of wisdom. The Bible puts it in these words:

> The fear of the LORD is the beginning of wisdom.
> — Proverbs 9:10

The fear of God does not involve cowering in terror with an ashen face. It is not shuddering with apprehension or trembling under impending doom. To "fear" God is to take him seriously. It is the awareness that God means what he says. It is choosing not to ig-trivialize, or minimize God's Word. It means believing God, not because we can figure everything out, but because we are certain the one who said it can back up every word. If we fear God, we don't even attempt to play foolish games with him, as if it didn't matter — because *it does*. Remember that behind every self-defeating behavior in our lives is a lie that we are believing. In order to stop defeating ourselves, we must first stop deceiving ourselves. That means taking God seriously and adjusting our thinking accordingly. It means being honest with God.

No relationship can survive, much less grow, if those involved in it are not honest with each other. God has been honest *with* us and *about* us. As we endeavor to move closer to God, we are continually confronted with new insights that demand an overhaul of our thinking. Unless we recalibrate our core concepts of life, our relationship with God will remain distant. By taking God seriously and facing up to the truth, we too can become honest in this relationship. In doing so, we remove some relational barriers. We stop arguing with God. We no longer waste time defending our personal perspectives on life. There is a refreshing freedom in the ability to admit that we are wrong and that God is right.

The Scriptures expose the truth about us and force us to be honest before God. Nothing escapes the exposing light of the Word. It goes to the core of our being, appraising both our soul and our spirit. The true status of our spiritual life is held up before us. What really goes on inside us as we relate to God and to this world cannot be hidden or disguised. All excuses vaporize. We are forced to be honest with God:

> For the word of God is living and active and sharper than any two-edged sword, and piercing as far as the division of soul and spirit, of both joints and marrow, and able to judge the thoughts and intentions of the heart. (Hebrews 4:12)

Our thoughts are included in the audit, along with the intentions that lurk behind them. We are confronted with the real bent of our heart — our passions, our deceptions, our motives, our intentions. The dramatic transformation God desires for us to experience comes from dramatic changes in our thinking. Romans 12:2 says that a transformed life is the result of a renewed mind, one that is no longer polluted with deadly philosophies.

By Genuinely Processing What God Says

> Solid food is for the mature, who because of practice have their senses
> trained to discern good and evil. (Hebrews 5:14)

Having indulged ourselves in God's Word and having determined
to take Yahweh seriously, we must become proactive in response to
what God has said. It is active, rather than passive, listening. Malcolm Muggeridge writes, "Future historians are likely to conclude
that the more we knew about Jesus the less we knew him, and the
more precisely his words were translated the less we understood or
heeded them."[5]

In order to avoid such an indictment, there are some basic questions that any disciple can, and should, ask in the course of a personal
study of God's Word. These questions can help turn seemingly irrelevant words on a page into practical, life-transforming concepts
for life. They draw us into the mind of God. The questions fall
into four categories: observation, personalization, implementation,
and integration.

Observation. God desires for us to know and understand his Word.
It is not God's intention to make his concepts for living difficult to
find. The Word is laid out in a format designed for common people.
God clearly spells things out, in bullet statements as in the Ten Commandments. But in order to make sure that we don't miss the point,
God provides us with accounts of how these concepts are to be
lived out, including the blessings of success and the consequences
of failure. Yahweh wraps them into songs and proverbs and parables.

If we are simply observant as we read the Scriptures, we will
never be lacking for insight. Several questions that can help in this
process are

- What is the theme, or main point, of this portion of Scripture?

- What are some of the lessons to be learned from this account?

- What is God revealing about himself in these verses?

Personalization. One of the biggest problems believers face in their
study of the Scriptures is an inability to connect practical life with
biblical principles. It helps to understand that, even though thousands of people have read the words of Scripture before, they are

God's personal conversation with each of us at this precise moment. The words of Scripture are not meaningless meanderings about irrelevant issues. They are a private discussion between the awesome God of the universe and God's trusted friend. The Bible is another opportunity to hear the voice of God. Some questions that might help in seeing the Scriptures this way are

- What are some of the issues in your life that are affected by what you have read in these verses?

- In what specific ways are these personal issues affected?

- What is God graciously revealing about you in order that you might come closer to him?

Implementation. Show time! This is where God's Word becomes visible, moving from the conceptual to the concrete. God does not promise blessings for merely knowing what his Word says. It is in the application of the Word that we experience the special benefits God has promised. Until we take action, we cannot honestly say that we are under the authority of God's Word. Several questions that can help activate the Scriptures are

- What are you going to do differently today because of what God has revealed to you in his Word?

- What will your new actions look like? How and when and why are you going to carry out your plan of action?

- How do you expect to see God involved in your life today?

Integration. Unless we come to conscious conclusions about what God has said about himself as Creator and us as his creation — unless we take what God has said and done and settle in our mind that it is true — we are doomed to repeat lesson after lesson in the same course. God is determined to have his children learn his truth and has given us the choice to learn either by insight or experience. But one way or the other, we will learn. A couple of questions that help in this process are

- What did you see God do in response to your obedience?

- What have you learned about God and yourself as a result of putting his Word into action?

Spiritual Savvy

As a result of giving God our full attention, taking him seriously, and processing what we hear, we have the opportunity to develop spiritual savvy. It is the practical result of delighting in the mind of God, a mind-set that harmonizes with God. The Bible refers to it as *wisdom*.

The wisdom that accompanies new life in Christ is the ability to consistently make choices that are pleasing to God because we have lived close enough to have learned what delights his heart (Ephesians 5:10). Wisdom is living by design rather than by default. It is understanding how life works, based upon what God has said, and proceeding accordingly. Wisdom includes insight and understanding and *un* common sense. It is the discernment and sound judgment of one who has the advantage of information accessible only to those who dare to come close to God and listen to his voice with their entire being. Such wisdom is not laced with ulterior motives or humanistic psychobabble. It resolves conflicts, personal and interpersonal, and does so in a nonabrasive way. Identified by compassion and positive results, wisdom is never outdated and cannot be faked. There are several unmistakable characteristics of spiritual savvy.

Eternal Perspective

Those who are spiritually savvy always appear to be living in light of a bigger picture. That's because they are! As wisdom matures, such people seldom get caught up in insignificant trivia or petty issues. They realize that this life is not all there is, that it is preparation for eternity. They are increasingly more aware that regardless of how things appear, there is always something bigger happening. Malcolm Muggeridge wrote,

> When I look back on my life...what strikes me most forcibly about it is that what seemed at the time most significant and seductive, seems now most futile and absurd. For instance, success in all of its various guises; being known and being praised; ostensible pleasures, like acquiring money or seducing women or traveling....In retrospect, all these exercises seem pure fantasy, what Pascal called, "licking the earth."[6]

The psalmist knew, as we must come to know, that there are no insignificant days in the lives of God's people:

> So teach us to number our days,
> That we may present to Thee a heart of wisdom.
> — Psalm 90:12

To "number a day" is to give it importance, to single out each day as having unique value. I recently did something that I would guess few people have ever done. I calculated exactly how many days I have been alive on this earth. On the day I did this, I figured I was living out my 16,947th day. It wasn't a particularly encouraging thought, especially when I considered how many of those days had probably been wasted on trivial matters that had nothing to do with eternity.

The spiritually savvy have a value system that expresses itself in a radically different arrangement of priorities. Over time, what is considered important is continuously refined and adjusted to match the weight assigned by the Scriptures. There is an eternal perspective.

Skillful Living

Those with spiritual savvy display a graceful skill in living. Because they know their way around, there is a confidence in their manner. As time progresses, they make the difficult mechanics of life look easy.

I have a niece who competed in the 1996 Olympics in Atlanta. Her event was rowing, and she won a silver medal in the women's doubles. Watching her compete was fun. There was the beauty of strength applied with graceful precision. The training plan for such competition had five steps: (1) Learn the basics and practice. (2) Develop strength and practice. (3) Learn to work as a team and practice. (4) Acquire the subtle skills and practice. (5) Then visualize winning and practice, practice, practice. I enjoyed seeing the obvious freedom they experienced in being able to present a virtually flawless performance. My respect stems from the realization of the intense discipline required to achieve their level of skill.

Many believers seem to live as though the Christian life were an impromptu free-for-all and are content to make the same awkward errors in living over and over again, and to remain on the level of a spiritual amateur. While the Christian life is not merely a performance, there is definitely a graceful skill in living that accompanies spiritual maturity. It is a quality referred to in the Bible as "godliness" and cannot be achieved by merely adding years to one's life. There are no simple shortcuts.

Good Judgment

Spiritual savvy is also seen in decision making, not only in what is decided but also in how a person arrives at the decision. Decisions will be bathed in prayer, based upon biblical concepts, and bounced off of a number of credible counselors. The decisions become less impulsive and less selfish. I once had a good friend tell me, "I have discovered that my first inclination is seldom God's best for me."

One of the most attractive benefits of wisdom is that it offers practical freedom from the dreaded curse of human stupidity. It presents a viable alternative to the foolishness of this world. No one likes to make stupid mistakes or live with the consequences of foolish decisions. It is true that we win or lose by the way we choose. There is no escaping the consequences of our choices. So a life marked by the wisdom of intimacy with sound judgment, skillful living, and a gracious attitude is attractive.

Conclusion

Do you have a private place where you meet with God and listen to God's voice? I am not referring to some mystical experience where you commune with nature and wait for an audible voice to break forth from somewhere in space. Do you have a place like where I sat with my grandfather, a place removed from other voices that demand your attention and distract you from the one you most urgently need to hear?

As you open the pages of the Bible, do you take a moment to think about who it is that is about to speak to you? Do you realize that God has prepared this moment from eternity past and that what you are about to hear is from the very mind and heart of Yahweh? Are you aware of God's desire for you to actually know more of him and to come closer because of what you find in those pages? Do you know that God so desired this closeness that he declared, "I will put My law within them, and on their heart I will write it" (Jeremiah

31:33)? And can you sense the deep delight of David when he cried, "O how I love Thy law!" (Psalm 119:97)?

Drawing Closer

1. How is your experience in God's Word affected by your relational proximity to Yahweh? How is your intimacy with God affected by your time in his Word?

2. When was the last time you were delighted by a new discovery in God's Word? What was it that you discovered?

3. What is one way your thinking (philosophies and perceptions) has changed as a result of being in the Scriptures? Has that change in thinking altered your experience of intimacy with God? How?

4. Can you see yourself in the "Bonsai" illustration? How can you alter that picture?

5. In what specific ways do you believe others might recognize spiritual savvy in you? Where might it show up best? Where might it be seen the least?

⟋ SEVEN ⟍

Venturing into the Heart of God

(seeing life through God's eyes)

O NE OF THE GREATEST RESCUES IN HISTORY OCCURRED ON MAY 25, 1991. It was carried out under the code name "Operation Solomon." Fourteen thousand Ethiopian Jews were airlifted from Addis Ababa to Tel Aviv:

> Chutzpah and meticulous planning was accompanied by plain bribery: 35 million dollars was reportedly handed over to make sure that the rescue went ahead as rebel forces advanced. Some of the Ethiopian officials involved in the shadier side of the deal got on the aircraft to escape with the departing Jews to the safety of Israel.
>
> The Falashas were "coming home" to a vastly different life from the one they had known in their native land. Most are unskilled farm laborers, already traumatized by being uprooted from their villages in Gonder and Tigre. Some have had to be shown how to use telephones or flush lavatories.[1]

Ruth Westheimer and Steven Kaplan described Operation Solomon in stark terms:

> Despite the inevitable discomfort of many of the passengers, the plane, which carried among its three hundred children a baby born only minutes before take off, was almost silent. Nor were the passengers particularly concerned with the in-flight meals (there were none), the fate of their luggage (even their carry-on was minimal), the in-flight movie (cartoons and El/Al publicity films), or the possibility of long lines at customs or passport control.... Fourteen thousand Ethiopian Jews arrived in Israel in less than thirty-six hours. Never had so many *olim* (immigrants) entered the country in so short a period.[2]

As you read this page, a far more amazing rescue is in progress, one that involves every creature ever formed by the hand of God, those in heaven and those on this planet. All creation feels the intensity of the drama. The cast includes an evil ruler and a horde of rebellious henchmen. There is a royal liberator leading a mighty force of righteous warriors. At stake are millions of oppressed souls who know little or nothing of the hideous peril awaiting them.

As the rescue unfolds, those who have been freed are returned as insurgents into the occupied territory in an effort to release the remaining captives. They are deployed throughout the evil empire as visible evidence that the freedom they have gained is permanent and powerful. They are not an underground movement but openly go about undermining the authority of the corrupt regime by living a countercultural lifestyle empowered by their Redeemer.

Reading the Pulse of God's Heart

As I stumble out of bed in the morning, chug down some coffee, and begin my trek through the day, it is not my natural inclination to view life in such dramatic terms. Most days have an earthy commonness to them. The people around me look normal and unconcerned, at least about spiritual things. They are not waiting for me to rescue them. In fact, they prefer that I mind my own business and leave them alone. But something happens to my perspective of the world when I move closer to God. My assessment of these common people living ordinary lives changes as I venture into the heart of God.

I have found that the more time I spend with someone, the more I will understand what is in that person's heart. As the relationship grows, I begin to recognize how the passions of the heart drive the actions of the person. Moving closer, standing where that person stands, I can see life from a new vantage point. Closer yet, and I can begin to feel the heartbeat; I can feel the passion itself. Still closer, and the passion becomes my own. Could it be that I do not aggressively carry out the rescue operation because I don't see life as God sees it? Is my heart so different from Yahweh's that it does not break to see people estranged from their Creator — people captives of an oppressor?

There are many how-to books out there dealing with the subject of evangelism. Training seminars and entire organizations are devoted to helping God's people become more adept at what should be, but isn't, a normal part of the Christian life. I do not wish to offer any critiques or improvements upon them. I would simply like to reinforce two elements of this graceful invasion that are vital to its success, two features of intimacy with God that are literally at the heart of the issue.

A Credible Life

The first of these elements is a credible life. Colossians 4:5–6 provides some insight concerning how we are to conduct ourselves around those who are presently outside the family of God, those who have not yet been rescued:

> Conduct yourselves with wisdom toward outsiders, making the most of the opportunity. Let your speech always be with grace, seasoned as it were, with salt, so that you may know how you should respond to each person.

Based upon these verses, a credible life means living on purpose. As we order our lives, we are to wisely consider how it will be perceived by the unbelieving world around us. We are called to live a well-thought-through life, one that provides visible evidence of our redemption. Understanding God's "big picture," we are to plan our actions accordingly. Haddon Robinson writes, "Outsiders to faith are first drawn to Christians and then to Christ."[3] In a similar vein, author Sheldon Vanauken says, "The best argument for Christianity is Christians; their joy, their certainty, their completeness. But the strongest argument against Christianity is also Christians — when they are somber and joyless, when they are self-righteous and smug in complacent consecration, when they are narrow and repressive, then Christianity dies a thousand deaths."[4]

We are to live not only *on* purpose but also *with* purpose. Each day is filled with opportunities to display the grace of God at work in our lives. These opportunities often take unusual and unexpected forms. We never know exactly what God will open before us. I have heard it said that we follow a Redeemer who is notoriously unpredictable.

One of the many examples of this in my life occurred years ago when my son decided he would like to play soccer. As a supportive father, I would walk with him to the practice field located just a couple of blocks away. I would watch the drills and cheer him on. Then we would walk home together, discussing the state of the team and our prospects for a winning season.

There were only a few parents who would stick around for the hour-long practices. One was another soccer dad, a genuinely nice guy who had gone through some pretty rugged experiences in his life. In fact, life was rather traumatic for him right at that time. I knew this because he told me all about it. As we stood at the edge of the lawn, watching kids chase soccer balls in all directions, this dad would talk nonstop.

At each practice, the soccer dad would pick up right where he left off last time. "So," he would begin, "remember what I was telling you the other day? Well guess what. ... " And the monologue would continue, each time getting deeper and more personal. He talked about his marriage, affairs, and finances. He expounded on his philosophies and on how things ought to be. I didn't mind at all. But it was funny because he had absolutely no idea whom he was talking to. In the wrong hands, the information he was divulging could destroy him. Yet the weeks went by, and he never asked one question about me, not even my name.

Unbeknownst to both of us, we had some mutual friends, a young couple in the church I was pastoring at the time. For years, they had been trying to get this soccer dad to come with them to church. Finally, in the midst of this soccer season, he agreed to give it a shot. Now, this young couple had a habit of sitting in the front row (my astronomy professor would be proud), and that is exactly where they ushered their reluctant friend. You can imagine the astonishment of this man as, moments later, his anonymous soccer buddy took center stage as the spiritual leader of the church.

In the subsequent weeks, our conversations changed. There was an obvious difference in how he viewed me. He began to refer to me as "pastor," asking for my advice concerning the issues in his life. He spent more time listening than talking. He had spent weeks expressing his needs and building a relational bridge. He had seen what he felt was a credible life, and now he was ready to hear some answers.

A Credible Answer

Alongside a credible life, there must be a second essential element: a credible answer. Paul says that our conversation should always be gracious. That is, it should show interest in others and draw them out of themselves. It should be marked by honest listening. These should be positive dialogues that build relationships and invite further discussion. But within any interaction involving a believer, there should be an element of salt. Peter added more insight to the "salt" portion of the conversation when he wrote,

> Sanctify Christ as Lord in your hearts, always being ready to make a defense to everyone who asks you to give an account for the hope that is in you, yet with gentleness and reverence. (1 Peter 3:15)

In order to have a credible answer, we must know what we believe and understand why we believe it. God clearly states that we are to be prepared to defend what we believe and to account for what has happened within us.

So, what do I believe? I believe that God exists. I believe that Yahweh is a personal God, the God of the Scriptures, who has revealed himself in nature and history. I believe that Jesus was God in the flesh. I believe that Christ lived, died, and rose again as recorded in the Bible. I once heard it said that if Jesus is not who he says he is, then nothing matters. We are free to do whatever we desire without any consideration to morality or ethics. But if Jesus *is* who he says he is, and if he *can* do what he says he can do, nothing *else* matters.

I believe that the sixty-six books of the Bible are God's words, the very breath of God. As such, I believe the Scriptures speak with authority, exposing reality about God, about me, and about life itself. I believe that God designed me to be in a personal relationship with him. I also believe that I am a sinner, just as the Bible says, and that Jesus died in my place that I might be forgiven. All my hope of ever being right with God I have placed in what Jesus did on the cross. And because of that, I believe I am a new person in Christ. I have been set free!

In addition to knowing what we believe, we must know why we believe what we do. Simply because we believe something doesn't make it true. The whys of our faith are an essential part of a credible answer. The only valid reason for anyone to believe what we present to them is because it's true. It should be intellectually sound and have philosophical integrity. There should be historical evidence to support it. And finally, it should bear itself out in our own personal experience. Jim Petersen refers to this as a congruent life: "A congruent life is the secret of naturalness in communication. And naturalness is the secret of attracting rather than repelling with our witness. On the other hand, where there are incongruities in our lives we usually have to resort to devises or gimmicks to get our message across."[5]

One of the most significant tools we have for communicating our evidence to a world oppressed by a spiritual dictator is our personal story of how we came to freedom in Christ. It is an account of the hope that is in us. While serving a church on the Oregon coast, I launched an experiment. I challenged people to write a clear, concise statement of how they came to know Jesus as Savior and of how he had changed their lives. I pulled together a team of editors to help believers put their testimonies into words that would communicate well. And here's the clincher. The finished product, along with a photograph, would be printed in the local newspaper.

To my amazement, we had no lack of takers. People responded to the challenge. Each week, they would report what had happened as a result of their article appearing in the newspaper. There were also some unexpected benefits for each of the participants. They found that as the publication date approached, they became increasingly aware of their own personal life. They felt a greater need for prayer, and they took time carefully to consider questions they might be asked. They became intensely aware of who they were and of what was at stake. They began to feel the pulse of God's heart.

Touching the Power of God's Heart

Our Father God has chosen to include each of his children in the master plan of redemption. Every individual who has been rescued from sin and found new life in Christ is to be actively involved in this

spiritual confrontation. William Temple captured this idea by accurately observing, "The church of Jesus Christ is the only cooperative
society that exists for the benefit of its non-members." The mission
statement of every collection of believers on earth is the same. We
exist for the purpose of glorifying God by leading people to Jesus
Christ and helping them grow in their relationship with him. That's
pretty straightforward. Its implementation calls for both a cultural
subversion and a personal invasion.

A Cultural Subversion

God has called us to live highly visible lives that prove who we are
as God's own redeemed people, lives that demand an explanation,
lives lived close to God. In doing so, we actually sabotage the philosophies, values, and attitudes that dominate the thinking of our present
generation. Paul wrote to the Roman believers,

> Do not be conformed to this world, but be transformed by the renewing
> of your mind, that you may prove what the will of God is, that which is
> good and acceptable and perfect. (Romans 12:2)

The subversive nature of an authentic Christian life has been
felt throughout history. "Consider the accusations that were brought
against the early Christians," writes Christian philosopher Jacques
Ellul. "In the relevant Roman texts they are regarded not merely
as 'enemies of the human race' but as atheists and destroyers of
religion. . . . It was 'antireligion.' This view was well-founded. What
the first Christian generations were putting on trial was not just the
imperial religion, as is often said, but every religion in the known
world."[6] What is more, by demonstrating the reality of new life in
Christ, we also put on trial every personal opinion, paradigm, and
philosophy of life held by those who observe how we live. In order
to carry out this mission effectively, we must have an understanding
of the current moral and ethical climate. Just because we live in a
culture doesn't mean that we understand it. I am a classic example
of the baby-boomer generation, but it took some concentrated effort
to actually figure out what a "boomer" was.

As David assembled his military team, he included a contingent
from the tribe of Issachar, "men who understood the times, with

knowledge of what Israel should do" (1 Chronicles 12:32). These were perceptive men who felt the pulse of their time. They understood what was going on in the minds of their peers, what motivated them and what frightened them, what were their interests and priorities in life. This same awareness is a key to reaching our own generation of captives.

We must also have an understanding of who we are in the midst of those times. The Bible describes us as aliens in a hostile environment, light in the darkness, and sheep among wolves. We are letters to be read and salt to be tasted. We are ambassadors and reconcilers. We are new creatures, people who have been raised from the dead, captives who have been set free. As those who claim to have discovered new life in Christ, we are to display that life in terms of a radically different lifestyle. We operate with a different philosophy and with different values.

A Personal Invasion

The spiritual rescue operation described at the beginning of this chapter requires an invasion of the personal privacy that is defended so passionately. Those apart from Christ guard their privacy out of self-preservation. Any intrusion into their personal lives could expose the desperate emptiness of spiritual death. It could deepen the agonizing realization of their loneliness, guilt, and hopelessness. Being in the presence of one who enjoys intimacy with God exposes their alienation from the Creator.

It is easy to be fooled by appearances, to think that those around us are happy, fulfilled, and confident. It is easy to think that we are the only ones who have ever found themselves sickened by the holocaust within. The truth is that everyone apart from Christ is just as lifeless and lonely as we once were — everyone. Apart from Christ, each one of us is enslaved to the despotic ruler of this earth and is being led on a death march to a very real and decidedly final destination, hell.

It is also true that we are a vital part of this liberation process. God has designed the plan in such a way that no one can escape on their own. Our part is to guide others to where salvation awaits them. As ones who have been proven to be authentically free and who know where the freedom is found, it is our responsibility to do everything possible to assist the captives in their escape. But the tyrannized need more than a guide if they are ever to experience freedom. Having convinced themselves that their present existence is the only legitimate one and that any talk of freedom is a hoax, the captives must experience a change of heart before they will follow a guide away from whatever security they cling to.

The only one who can accomplish the change in the core of a person is God. No amount of convincing arguments from the guide can do it. Such a personal invasion involves drawing the hearts of people toward the heart of God. It calls for communicating the love God has for them, a love we have personally experienced. There is, however, no guarantee of how it will be received. That part is in the hands of God.

Elizabeth Barrett Browning is known for her beautiful literature, much of which is in the form of love letters, but there is a sad story behind those letters. Elizabeth's parents were vehemently against her marriage to Robert, so much so that they disowned her. In an effort to renew the relationship with her parents, Elizabeth wrote love letters to them. She continued this on a weekly basis for almost ten years. Then one day she received a large parcel in the mail. When she opened it, her heart was broken. Within the box were all the letters she had written. Not one of them had ever been opened.[7]

As those who know the love of God personally, who have pored over his love letters and absorbed their truth, it is now up to us to communicate that love to those around us. We cannot force them to open the letters, but we *can* ensure that they are never lacking a letter to read.

Experiencing the Passion of God's Heart

Of all the biblical instructions for the life of a believer, it seems that the one that strikes the most fear in the hearts of God's people is the one that calls them into the heat of battle as spiritual guerrillas. Admittedly, there are legitimate grounds for fear. To carry out the mission, we must be willing to step beyond where we feel comfortable and put relationships at risk. While an excitement and adventure come with our participation in the rescue, those same words can also be restated in terms of fear.

Now, I do not want to sound too simplistic or artificially spiritual, but it is true that our relationship with God is what overcomes the fear of speaking to others about salvation. There we find both the motivation for evangelism and the means for drawing others to the longing of their hearts. And there is more. When we engage ourselves in the mission, we discover a secret passageway into the heart of God.

Evangelism is one activity that has a direct and profound effect on the depth of our walk, the realization of our freedom, and the tuning of our hearts. I once heard someone say that the Christian life without evangelism is like a can of Coke that has been opened and left on the counter overnight. All that remains is a syrupy sweetness. It loses all its fizz. Spiritual passion comes from venturing into the heart of God. Consider some very substantial reasons why involvement in evangelism is essential to intimacy with God.

First, evangelism affects the depth of our walk by forcing us to address the issues of life and discover real answers to the questions posed by those who are yet hostile to the gospel. Our involvement in the rescue operation defies the possibility of wallowing in shallowness. We cannot get by with trite buzzwords and phrases and in-house lingo. We must be able to bring authentic answers to real questions — the questions that those around us are really asking. Author Rebecca Pippert writes that apart from Christ "all we feel is a certain wordless sadness deepened by simplistic solutions that trivialize our problems and insult our intelligence. In short, it is hard to live too long before we start asking, Is there something missing or wrong with our lives? Where do we go to find lasting happiness, and where is the power to help us reach it?"[8]

Answering the questions of unbelievers forces us deeper into God's Word. It may mean that we must wrestle with a question far more than the one who posed it to us. The question may touch some of our own uncertainties and press us to settle some issues that lie unresolved within ourselves. But with each answer we find our own faith strengthened. With each new insight we experience greater confidence in God's Word and greater confidence in its Author.

Second, evangelism affects the realization of our freedom by making us aware of the fact that our lives are being watched. We become more sensitive to how our words, our actions, and our attitudes confirm or deny the freedom we claim to possess. We are compelled to put up or shut up. We find a positive incentive to live the truth of God's Word in unmistakably real life. In doing so, we discover more of the very freedom we want others to experience. It is a release from what Rebecca Pippert calls "our addiction to ourselves."[9] This freedom results from drawing close to the Liberator.

Third, evangelism affects the tuning of our hearts by matching our own thoughts and energies to those of God. The Almighty is passionate about the rescue, and as we immerse ourselves in the pursuit of his heart's desire, we find our own hearts becoming like Yahweh's. God's love for the lost becomes our love. God's awesome joy in their rescue becomes our own overwhelming joy.

Conclusion

In *Lifestyle Evangelism*, author Joseph C. Aldrich recounts a legend that tells the story of Jesus' return to glory after his time on earth:

> Even in heaven He bore the marks of His earthly pilgrimage with its cruel cross and shameful death. The angel Gabriel approached Him and said, "Master, you must have suffered terribly for men down there."
>
> "I did," He said.
>
> "And," continued Gabriel, "do they know all about how you loved them and what you did for them?"
>
> "Oh, no," said Jesus, "not yet. Right now only a handful of people in Palestine know."
>
> Gabriel was perplexed. "Then what have you done," he asked, "to let everyone know about your love for them?"
>
> Jesus said, "I've asked Peter, James, John, and a few more friends to tell other people about Me. Those who are told will in turn tell still other people about Me, and My story will be spread to the farthest reaches of the globe. Ultimately, all of mankind will have heard about My life and what I have done."
>
> Gabriel frowned and looked rather skeptical. He knew well what poor stuff men were made of. "Yes," he said, "but what if Peter and James and John grow weary? What if the people who come after them forget? What if way down in the twentieth century, people just don't tell others about you? Haven't you made any other plans?"

And Jesus answered, "I haven't made any other plans. I'm counting on them."[10]

God has chosen to involve us in his rescue operation, not because God cannot do it alone, but because the task intimately involves us in the passions of his heart. Apart from this activity, we cannot know the passion of God on a personal level. It is here that we begin to see life through God's eyes.

Drawing Closer

1. What is your greatest fear in sharing your faith with another person? What does that fear reveal about the state of your relationship with God?

2. What should be one's primary motivation to bring others into a saving re-lationship with God? How does intimacy with God affect the development of that motivation?

3. Why is intimacy with God so crucial in making a credible presentation of the gospel? What difference does it make?

4. How does the story of Elizabeth Browning apply to the unfolding salvation stories in your own life?

5. What in the visible nature of your relationship with God would make someone want to know him? Does your relationship with God make others envious? Why or why not?

Part 3

The
Dramatic
Discovery

(So this is what happens
when I draw close to God!)

─◌ EIGHT ◌─

Marked for Life

(giving your heart away)

O NE OF THE MOST SIGNIFICANT QUESTIONS EVER POSED TO JESUS was asked by a man who thought he had all the answers. He was a lawyer, an expert in Jewish law. It was supposed to be a trick question intended to trap Jesus in some legal snare of spiritual controversy. The Gospel writers record the incident from differing vantage points.[1] In doing so, they captured the importance of the question. It was asked in light of what was the most impressive feature of knowing God, the most dramatic expression of life, and the most striking characteristic of the Kingdom. Jesus was asked which was the greatest of all the commandments. His answer:

> " 'Love the Lord your God with all your heart and with all your soul and with all your mind.' This is the first and greatest commandment. And the second is like it: 'Love your neighbor as yourself.' All the Law and the Prophets hang on these two commandments." (Matthew 22:37–40, NIV)

In the days when Jesus walked the earth, the Greeks had refined their vocabulary of love to communicate its various facets. There was, for example, a specific term to describe a general love for humankind. It was the kind of love that creates a sense of compassion for flood victims in a Midwest farm town or for starving tribes in some dusty desert plain in Africa. Another term captured the kind of love that welds a family together. It communicated the natural affection between a husband and wife, between parents and children. Still another word was employed to express the bond between friends. Wrapped into its meaning were the various levels of closeness that are developed from common experiences or shared interests. It conveyed the enjoyment of people and included everything from a casual acquaintance to a kindred spirit. And then, of course, yet another term conveyed the sensual emotions one has for a lover. This was a term of romance and passion, one that responded to something of beauty in another person. Such love moved the poets and supplied material for love songs.

Each of these terms added color and dimension to the experiences we know as love. None of them was considered superior to the other, and while all of these elements of love should be found among believers, they fall short of describing the powerful love that bonds us both to God and to God's people. Each word focused attention on a type of relationship. In each case, something evoked a response of love. Whether it was blood, beauty, or benefits, in each word there was something that moved the heart and made one want to respond to a person.[2]

Yet another "love" word was in circulation at the time. It was a less common word, one that emphasized the commitment of love rather than its emotion — a term heavy on responsibility without regard to the rewards. It conveyed the solid bedrock of love, the foundation upon which all other aspects of love must be built if they are to withstand the punishing blows of the imperfect people we love. It was the word *agape* (ä-**gä**-pay). God selected this word to describe the core of our relationship with him and with others.

Agape was an impact word that meant to cultivate closeness apart from any kinship or attractiveness in the person to be loved. It was marked by a commitment of the will to cherish and uphold another person, a decision to treat someone with concern and care and thoughtfulness, and a commitment to work for that person's best interests. Such love was an action, rather than a reaction, a decision to make that person a "somebody" by placing a high value on the individual. Agape was relational impact.

What was true in biblical times is just as true today. People around us are very familiar with family love and philanthropic love. They are well acquainted with the bonds of friendship and the passion of romance. But most often they have known these facets of love apart from the foundation of agape and certainly apart from the hybrid agape love of the Scriptures.

We live in a world where everything has a price tag and everyone seems to have a "hidden agenda." When someone carries out an unsolicited act of kindness or has a particularly pleasant demeanor, we tend to wonder what such a person really wants. It seems inconceivable that someone would behave in such a manner without expecting something in return. We conclude that the person must be selling something or looking for special favors.

In the Bible, agape love is refined and given its own detailed description. While the ancient Roman world provided the basic word, God recast it with his own definition. As this love was lived out by Christians in the practical settings of daily life, it not only made an impact upon its recipients; it jolted an observing world. It was, and still is, impressive to find someone who genuinely cares about others and is willing to invest in them unselfishly, someone who is willing to give away his or her heart, rather than to protect it. A second-century Church Father by the name of Tertullian documented the impact of this love with these words, "It is mainly the practice of such love that leads some to put a brand on us. 'See,' they say, 'how these Christians love one another! . . . And how ready they are to die for one another!' "[3]

Love is indeed the premier mark of our connectedness to God (1 John 4:7–21; Galatians 5:22). It is the one and only evaluation of authenticity that God has placed in the hands of unbelievers. Jesus announced both a blessing and a curse when he told his disciples, "By this all men will know that you are My disciples, if you have love for one another" (John 13:35).

With this declaration, the world has been given the right to determine the truth of our claims on the basis of visible love. "This is the whole point," writes Francis Schaeffer. "The world is going to judge whether Jesus has been sent by the Father on the basis of something that is open to observation."[4] Biblical love is the greatest single factor in establishing our credibility as God's people. But just what is the unbelieving world supposed to see?

How Is a Believer's Life Marked?

The relational impact of biblical love is not out of reach for any believer. Agape is not simply an ideal to shoot for. God has made this centerpiece of intimacy a doable thing, but doable only for those who have experienced new life in Christ. Remember, it is *the* mark of the true follower of Christ.

By Receiving God's Love

The first step toward maturing in agape love is one of receiving. The Scriptures connect our ability to love others to our relationship with God. In other words, before we can express love, we must experience love. First John 4:19 says, "We love, because He first loved us."

Loving others is the result of being loved by God. We don't increase our love for others merely by trying harder to love them. Inevitably, we will find ourselves getting tripped up by their faults and failures. We will find reasons not to love them. We grow in our love for others by growing in our love relationship with God. The more we experience God's love, the more our heart is given the capacity to love others. The more we become acquainted with how God loves us, the more we know how to love others. In Ephesians 3:17–19, Paul prays,

> That Christ may dwell in your hearts through faith; and that you, being rooted and grounded in love, may be able to comprehend with all the saints what is the breadth and length and height and depth, and to know the love of Christ which surpasses knowledge, that you may be filled up to all the fulness of God.

The apostle Peter then applies this by writing,

> Since you have in obedience to the truth purified your souls for a sincere love of the brethren, fervently love one another from the heart. (1 Peter 1:22)

Experiencing God's love has a transforming effect. In love, God addresses each of the issues in our lives that cause us to act like jerks. Yahweh lovingly confronts arrogant attitudes and conceited opinions of how we think we should be treated. God sets us free to love others by setting us free from the love of ourselves. "The visible evidence of maturity is relating in love," notes Larry Crabb. "As people learn to love, the internal structures that sustain their emotional and psychological ills are eroded. Love really *is* the answer. It is the defining mark of the Christian."[5]

Before we can deal with how others have mistreated us, we must experience God's love covering our own failures. Until we realize how unlovable we are, we cannot respond appropriately to God's love. As we give God freedom to expose our sin in all its ugliness, as we become increasingly aware of just how much God must tolerate in us, it becomes easier to forgive and tolerate others. Before we can draw the best out of others, we must experience the love of God developing the character of Jesus in us. It is, in fact, that very character we will find ourselves searching for in others. And it is those qualities that we will long to see emerging from other people.

By Responding to God's Love

While the first step is one of receiving God's love, the second is one of responding to it. That response becomes tangible as we take the love we have received from God and direct it toward others. "Love is as love does," writes author Jerry Jenkins. "Love is not a state of being. It's an act of the will. It cannot be demanded or required or commanded. It can only be bestowed."[6] Agape must be expressed before it can be authentic:

> By this we know that we love the children of God, when we love God and observe His commandments. (1 John 5:2)

Some people are easy to love. There are people to whom we are attracted by their physical appearance and their personality. We are drawn to those who have similar interests, who pursue similar goals, and who often have the same taste in a variety of life's choices. We find them lovable people. We enjoy being around them, and it is not a chore to invest in them or to make sacrifices on their behalf. They are people who draw out the best in us, people with whom we feel at ease. When the Bible commands us to love these people... no problem!

There are others, a rather large tribe of them, who are not so easy to love. The more people differ from us, the more difficult it is to love them. And since the world is populated by people who are different, most of them will provide a challenge for love. Individual quirks and flaws of personality are part of the package. Some are high-maintenance people who consume enormous amounts of time and energy. With others, we may struggle to find points of commonness. It is easy to ignore such people, seeing them as tedious. But the Bible commands us to love these people too.

There are those who are lovely, others who are unlovely, and still others who are downright ugly. Into everyone's life come those who seem to have a personal mission statement that includes something about making your life miserable. They look for the worst in you. What they find, they expose; what they don't find, they invent. Conversations with such people are like walking through a minefield. They seem to defy love. And yet God specifically points to them and commands that they be loved.

A friend of mine spent the earliest years of her life in an orphanage. She has vivid memories of standing at a window and watching prospective parents arrive at the facility and of making snap decisions about them. There was a humiliating routine of having the children file in and stand before these clients, who would then point out which kids they would like to interview. Desperate as she was for a sense of closeness and connectedness, this young girl was not willing to entrust her heart to just anyone. So, if my friend liked what she saw in these people, she would brush her hair, stand up straight, and smile with all she had. But if, on the other hand, her first impressions were not favorable, she would muss her hair, slouch, and scrunch her face into a frown that said, "Keep out!" She told me that the latter half of this technique worked every time. As for the smile strategy ... well, ...

Agape love is not to remain an untested concept. We don't love people with good intentions. In the sixteenth century, Francis of Sales wrote, "You learn to speak by speaking, to study by studying, to run by running, to work by working; and just so, you learn to love God and man by loving."[7] Loving others is the confirming evidence that we have experienced God's love. If our experience of God's love is shallow, our love for others with be just as thin.

The Look of Love

Love is, by far, the easiest indicator of spiritual life to describe. The Scriptures are filled with observable reference points. The picture is clearly focused, and God leaves no room for confusion. There can be no question in our minds about whether or not we are acting in love.

As with any indicator of spiritual life, the starting point is Jesus. He was a living, breathing template for love. He spent time with people and never made them feel they were imposing on him. He constantly showed mercy to those who were in need. He laughed with them and cried with them.[8]

Jesus didn't condemn people for their failures but offered forgiveness. He brought hope into hopeless situations. He made people feel significant. The only ones who ever felt uncomfortable around Jesus were the self-righteous, those who felt they were already "somebodies." He was patient with twelve of the most difficult men on earth: greedy traitors, militant rebels, feisty fishermen. All of them were selfish and preoccupied with trivia, just like you and me.

The love modeled by Jesus was sacrificial. He willingly gave up his time and his privacy. He freely laid aside his divine titles and prerogatives. He forfeited many of the legitimate pleasures and comforts within his reach. Ultimately, he sacrificed his very life, dying in our place for our sin. Through all of this, Jesus never demonstrated the slightest resentment over what it cost him.

Missing the Point

Moving through the detailed description of love as it is presented in the Bible can be overwhelming and even discouraging. We can easily dismiss it all as simply an ideal toward which to aspire rather than as something attainable in real life. However, if that were true, God would never command such a thing. God would never stake the credibility of the Kingdom on something that was impossible for its citizens to accomplish.

Part of the glitch is in our perception of what is expected of us. We tend to think that if we are not presently doing these things, if we cannot imagine them fitting into our current pattern of living, and if we cannot see these qualities of love matching up with what we know about ourselves, then they are not realistic. It is perhaps with these factors in mind that we dilute the biblical concept of love, selectively choosing which characteristics we will emphasize and which we will ignore. We miss the point of agape. It is to signal a *changed* life, one that visibly displays the presence of the living God.

Loving in Everyday Life

"Our ability to give and respond to love is our greatest gift," observe authors Henry Cloud and John Townsend. "The heart that God has fashioned in his image is the center of our being. Its abilities to open up to love and to allow love to flow outward are crucial to life."[9] As this heart is activated, God's love is put into inescapably graphic terms. In 1 Corinthians 13:4–8, we find a concentrated dosage of applied agape — of giving away our heart:

> Love is patient, love is kind, and is not jealous; love does not brag and is not arrogant, does not act unbecomingly; it does not seek its own, is not provoked, does not take into account a wrong suffered, does not rejoice in unrighteousness, but rejoices with the truth; bears all things, believes all things, hopes all things, endures all things. Love never fails.

These sixteen observable characteristics of love can be divided into three basic statements, three easily recognized forms of behavior that identify a kind of love that is rarely seen in this world. They are played out in the basic settings of life: in the home, in the workplace, and among other believers.

First: When we act in love, we choose not to act like a jerk. Simply put, a "jerk" is someone who is rude, crude, and ill-mannered. Reading through the description of love, did you notice how many of the elements are stated in negative terms? At least five of these could be subpoints placed under the general heading, "Thou shalt not be a jerk."

In terms of lifestyle, this statement means that as we grow in love, we become less preoccupied with ourselves. We decide not to use others in our desperate pursuit of significance. We don't demand that others admire and praise us, and we determine not to allow ourselves the freedom of an unquestioned jealousy when we are overlooked or when praise goes to someone else. We commit ourselves to resisting the urge to upstage others by bragging about ourselves. We will have a decreasing expectation that others will adjust to us and make up for what we fail to do.

Perhaps the word from 1 Corinthians 13 that best captures the actions of a jerk is the term "unbecoming." It refers to actions that cause another to feel uncomfortable, embarrassed, or in some way cheapened. Unbecoming behavior blurs the view of the finer qualities in a person that make him or her uniquely beautiful. It stifles the expression of those qualities by hoarding attention and diverting praise that might otherwise find its way to someone else.

There are many socially acceptable and sadly common expressions of unbecoming actions that are both subtle and devastating. Among them is the failure to show courtesy. Insensitive jokes and careless comments belittle what is important to the one who is said to be the object of love. Complaining and nagging also fit into this category. But perhaps one of the most unbecoming actions of all is indifference — shutting off someone as though that person were unimportant, uninteresting, or unneeded.

Love, on the other hand, conducts itself in a way that draws attention to the beautiful qualities in another person, attributes that might otherwise go unnoticed. It takes the form of private compliments and public praise. In the same way that becoming clothes make the wearer look good, becoming behavior can make others look good. It involves actions that allow another not only to feel comfortable but even highly prized and important. Love never gives a reason for someone to lose a sense of worth.

Second: When we act in love, we choose not to be offended. While the first of these agape characteristics keeps us from driving others away, the second checks our own pulling away from those around us. The New Testament word for "forgiveness" carries the idea of removing an obstacle, of sending it away, of not taking it into account. By forgiving someone, we are releasing our grip on whatever has offended us. We are choosing not to force the offender to pay for his or her actions. We are not going to retaliate or punish the offender to appease our own sense of justice. Forgiveness means that we are not going to define the relationship in terms of the offense. Instead, we are going to base it upon something bigger, looking past the offense to a point of reconciliation. Forgiveness means that we are committing ourselves to resolving the issues at stake in order to prevent any recurrence of an offense. Biblical love is seen in the refusal to allow the failures of another to destroy a relationship. It is determined grace that relentlessly pursues one who has fallen.

As we grow in our relationship with Christ, forgiveness increasingly becomes a natural extension of agape love. We become less demanding in the process of forgiveness. Because agape is not based upon the performance of its object, forgiveness can be unconditional. While we cannot erase the past from memory, we *can* choose not to dwell upon it in the present. We can choose not to embellish our memory with imagined motives and melodramatic replays.

Forgiveness also becomes easier as we choose not to "rejoice in unrighteousness." When acting in love, we don't get enjoyment from the failures of others. There is, instead, a grief over the sin in their lives. We are acting in love when we delight in weaving the truth of God's Word into every relationship. When we celebrate each step of faith in the life of another, then we are acting in love.

It should be noted that if we are loving others, we are not going to be easily provoked. That means that as we grow in love, we will become less irritable, not so easily bothered by the imperfections of life. We won't give ourselves the luxury of retreating into a grumpy mood. When we have been wronged, we won't start making plans to retaliate. We won't keep mental records of all the ways others have hurt us. In short, there is far less to forgive. Such a way of life stands out in a world where everything is the fault of someone else.

Tolerance is first among the qualities of agape (1 Corinthians 13:4). The word for patience means "long-suffering." In other words, it means putting up with those things in other people that irritate and annoy us and to do so without giving up on them. It is a quiet acceptance of God's unique plan and perfect timing for others. Patient love never doubts that God is at work in others, even when there is no visible evidence of it.

The people I appreciate most in my life are those who see my weaknesses most clearly and yet choose to cover them. They know exactly where the cracks and chips are but always draw the attention of others to my more polished qualities. They are people who refuse to let me remain as I am and yet have nothing but praise for me in the presence of others. They are people who speak openly with me about my areas of need but are quick to silence others who may speak of those areas to discredit me. They know the darkest of my secrets, and with them that information is safe.

Third: When we act in love, we choose to accentuate what is good. Our proximity to God can be gauged by the extent to which we search for the best in others. It is a tenacious pursuit of God's character in them and the celebration of what is found. Love makes it easy for others to change and to do what is right. This concept is captured in the five absolutes at the end of Paul's description of love.

"Love...bears all things" is testimony to an expanding ability to withstand whatever others may throw at us. We find ourselves less intimidated by the rubble in their lives. Love protects what is weak in another. It refuses to spread bad news about someone, while privately confronting him or her about personal weaknesses and failures. Love chooses to focus attention on where Jesus has triumphed, rather than on where people have failed.

"Love...believes all things." As love grows, so does our willingness to trust and to grant another chance. Love refuses to make another's failures terminal and is willing to accept the risk of being hurt again. There is, after all, no such thing as risk-free love.

"Love...hopes all things." Love supplies perpetual optimism to relationships. No one is hopeless in love's eyes. Love expects the best in the face of the worst. It sees people in light of God's promises.

"Love...endures all things." Love refuses to give up. It's not looking for an escape route. Love shares the weight in order to keep another from being crushed under it.

"Love never fails." It is never used up. The more it is employed, the more there is. If we are acting in love, we are willing to sacrifice our own desires and comforts in order to make others successful — in order to fulfill their dreams.

Such love has a price tag. It is sacrificial by its very nature. C. S. Lewis once observed,

> To love at all is to be vulnerable. Love anything, and your heart will certainly be wrung and possibly be broken. If you want to make sure of keeping it intact, you must give your heart to no one, not even to an animal. Wrap it carefully round with hobbies and little luxuries; avoid all entanglements; lock it up safe in the casket or coffin of selfishness. But in that casket — safe, dark, motionless, airless — it will change. It will not be

broken; it will become unbreakable, impenetrable, irredeemable.... The only place outside of Heaven where you can be perfectly safe from all the dangers ... of love is Hell.[10]

A Tale of Transformation

There once was a man who fell in love with a woman. There is nothing new about that except that this particular man was known for being angry and cruel. Life had dealt him many painful blows, and he had felt the full measure of each misfortune. Over the years, the anger inside him had brought villainous contortions to his face. It had come to the point where even his smile had an ominous cast to it. People kept their distance from him. There was always the fear that his hateful gaze might fall upon them and that he might lash out with unpredictable fury.

But when he met this beautiful maiden, his icy heart melted, and the anger within him dissipated. Life no longer seemed to have the same sting to it. He no longer saw life as something to be endured. The very thought of her took all the force from his former cruelty. The hardness was gone. He was most certainly a different man.

But the years had left their mark upon him. How could he possibly win this woman's heart? Such a beautiful maiden as this would never consider loving such a man as he. After all, he was who he was; wasn't he? His voice, his face, and his history all mocked at the longing of his heart. He could try to change his behavior to reveal the change in his heart, and he would. He could try to alter his words, along with the tones and inflections that carried them. But his face — now *there* was an obvious drawback to any romantic aspirations.

Determined to win her heart, this man did what any prospective hero in a fictional story would do. He sought out a master mask-maker and commissioned him to fashion a mask that matched his heart. The crafted disguise was a masterpiece, an exquisite facade with the noble form of a magnificent prince. So perfect was the craftsmanship that no one could detect its presence. And, indeed, the mask was a true representation of his heart.

Years passed, and the plan accomplished its intention. As the young woman considered the compassionate features of his face and gazed into his loving eyes, her heart was drawn to his. She fell in love. But with the romantic conquest came a painful realization. He was an impostor. She had fallen in love with the face of another man. For this love to be genuine, he would have to remove the mask. She would need to see him as he really was. Could she love the man behind the mask?

Choosing his time and words carefully, he came to his moment of truth. One more time he spoke of his love for her. And then, with trembling hands and a heart expecting to break, he slowly removed the mask. As he did so, he studied her expression, anticipating shock and disgust to overwhelm her. But it didn't. In fact, the same adoring eyes continued to blink back at him.

Confused, he found a mirror, and peering into it, he was stunned by the sight. He found himself looking at a face that matched the mask. The years of loving actions had brought his heart to the surface. His appearance had been transformed by his heart.[11]

We, too, are changed from the inside out. As our hearts are renewed by the love of God, the tack of our behavior, the tone of our conversation, and the very landscape of our faces are gradually conformed to the image of the Great Prince. New life in Christ invariably displays itself in love. It is the most impressive feature of knowing God, the most dramatic expression of life, and the most striking characteristic of the Kingdom. Biblical love is unmistakably visible, irresistibly attractive, and boundless in its expansion.

The closer we move toward God, the more we experience his awesome love. The more we experience his love, the more we are set free to express that love to others. The more we express that love, the more we authenticate our relationship to God. We confirm it not only to an observing world but also to ourselves.

Drawing Closer

1. List five reasons why God (or anyone else) would not want to love you. Why *does* God love you?

2. What is your "favorite" excuse for not loving others? How does God's presence affect that excuse?

3. Describe one way your manner of loving others is changing as you move closer to God.

4. Describe one way you have recently experienced God's love toward you. How has that changed your thinking, your attitude, your self-esteem? How has that experience changed how you love others?

5. Explain one way you have chosen to love someone who was difficult to love. Why did you choose to do so?

NINE

Intimate I-sight

(becoming real in an unreal world)

T WO PRIMARY PERSPECTIVES ON LIFE WERE CAPTURED IN THE CAR-
toon strip *Pickles*. Picture it with me. The first frame opens with
a frumpy old woman dressed in a bowling shirt, Bermuda shorts, and
slippers calling her dog to dinner, "Chow time, Roscoe." The pudgy
little mutt, with an endearing expression, considers his circumstance
in life as a bowl is placed before him, "She feeds me every day and
cares for my every need." Then, in the next frame, with the big round
eyes of amazement, he concludes, "She must be a god."

The cartoon strip continues by repeating the first frame. Only this
time a cat is being fed. "And here's yours, Muffin," the woman kindly
says to an overweight pet who is sporting a rather arrogant expression.
The feline considers the same situation, "She feeds me every day and
cares for my every need." But the conclusion is different, "*I* must
be a god."[1]

Probably the last thing you expected from this book was to be
categorized in some kind of animal group, but it may well be true
that humanity *is* composed of "dog" people and "cat" people. There
are those who stand in awe of God's goodness and are humbled
by God's gracious provision. But others (a much larger group) feel
that life owes them something, that somehow they are the center of
their universe.

C. S. Lewis wrote,

> There is one vice of which no man in the world is free; which every
> one in the world loathes when he sees it in someone else; and of which
> hardly any people, except Christians, ever imagine that they are guilty
> themselves.... There is no fault which makes a man more unpopular, and

> no fault which we are more unconscious of in ourselves. And the more we
> have it ourselves, the more we dislike it in others. The vice I am talking
> of is Pride or Self-Conceit; and the virtue opposite it, in Christian morals,
> is called Humility.[2]

Apart from Christ, life is filled with self-hyphenated characteristics. Terms like *self-centered*, *self-willed*, and *self-righteous*, along with *self-importance*, *self-indulgence*, and *self-pity*, dominate our personal resume. In other words, everything is about one's own self. What one thinks and what one feels are the most important factors in one's decisions. It is one's own preferences, one's own perspectives, one's own needs, and one's own interests that drive one's actions.

Drawing close to the Savior changes the orbit of our lives. This paradigm shift falls under the heading of humility. The biblical word for "humility" literally means "to be brought down" or "to be leveled." While at first blush it may appear rather undesirable, it is actually a very attractive virtue. Humility is a word that describes freedom from a me-magnetized life. Humility replaces those self-hyphenated characteristics with words like *unpretentious*, *unassuming*, and *unobtrusive*. Humility is personal honesty put into practical terms, a visual expression of intimacy with God.

How Does Intimacy Generate Humility?

Intimidating Humility

Humility has long been presented as an elusive quality. I have often been confused and frustrated by the double-talk that seems to be generated by many Bible teachers. According to them, humility is to be present in believers but never acknowledged. It is almost as though one must sneak up on humility and catch it by surprise. If one dares to openly pursue it, that person is embarking on a frustrating journey to a location that most biblical cartographers do not even identify on a map.

Humility seems an impossible task. On one hand, we are instructed to maintain a humble attitude (1 Peter 5:5–6) and to walk humbly with our God (Micah 6:8). We are told that our intimacy with God is governed by this quality (2 Chronicles 7:14). We are encouraged to search for others who possess humility and become known by our association with them (Proverbs 16:19). But, on the other hand, we are told that if we ever think we *are* humble, we're not.

The biblical mandate for personal humility is precise and pointed:

> He has told you, O man, what is good;
> And what does the LORD require of you
> But to do justice, to love kindness,
> And to walk humbly with your God?
> (Micah 6:8)

As those who have been chosen of God, holy and beloved, put on a heart of . . . humility. (Colossians 3:12)

Humble yourselves under the mighty hand of God. (1 Peter 5:6)

And if that isn't enough, consider the alternative:

The LORD detests all the proud of heart. (Proverbs 16:5, NIV)

Whoever exalts himself shall be humbled. (Matthew 23:12)

God opposes the proud but gives grace to the humble. (James 4:6, NIV)

It is apparent that God considers humility to be a basic element, rather than an optional attitude, in our spiritual health. It is also evident that humility does not come preinstalled in the "salvation package." God makes it very clear that it is our responsibility to produce it, cultivate it, and maintain it. But what motivates us to do so?

Intimate Humility

A significant difference exists between those who are soft-spoken and gentle by nature and those who are humble as a consequence of knowing the Master. It is possible to possess a nonabrasive personality while missing the dynamics of biblical humility. The two primary issues at the core of the biblical model are honesty and authority. The issue of honesty addresses who we are and who we are not. The issue of authority addresses who is in control and who is not.

Beginning, then, with the matter of honesty, we must direct attention to the truth about ourselves. Author Joseph Stowell writes, "Here is true humility, a proper attitude about ourselves that comes from understanding the greatness of God, our value before Him, and our inadequacy apart from Him."[3] If we simply compare ourselves to other people, our devious hearts will always be looking for ways to make ourselves come out on top. We all have flaws of character, and they are not difficult to spot. From the earliest stages of life, we become masters at honing in on the weaknesses in others in order to keep our own self-esteem intact. Apart from Christ, we have nothing with which to compare ourselves except other people. Thus, we will always be prone to pride and arrogance. But as we build intimacy with Christ, we find ourselves face-to-face with God, and a new comparison takes place.

Personal honesty can be very painful. We can be offended by the unflattering exposure of the process. However, what offends an individual reveals a great deal about that person. It is often some fortress of pride that has been assaulted or some weakness that has been exposed. There is a way we like to see ourselves (which is the way we want others to see us), and then there is the truth. One of the greatest levelers in life is a blunt collision with the evil that resides within us. The painful repercussions of personal failure and the torment of deserved guilt are often necessary to bring us down to earth. They rip apart our self-deceptions and ridicule our self-righteousness. Speaker and author Joni Eareckson Tada has written the bottom-line statement: "When it comes to gaining humility, the point is not to win but to lose. And our pride loses big when it goes up against God.... If we're looking for humility, we don't gaze inward to see how widely we've missed the mark. We gaze at God."[4]

As believers moving closer to God, we become increasingly more aware that life is not about us. It's about Yahweh. The larger God becomes in our minds and hearts, the smaller and more insignificant we become in our own estimation. In the beginning, this phenomenon is like seeing a magnificent mountain from a great distance. It can have little effect upon us. We may know its name and precise elevation. We may know its ancient history, as well as what kind of life exists upon it today. We may appreciate it as a feature of the larger landscape. We are fascinated by what we know but are not dwarfed by its reality. If we move closer, however, it becomes more impressive and takes up more of our view. If we continue to its very foot, we are overwhelmed as we gaze up at its awesome majesty. In all of this, the mountain hasn't changed. But our proximity to it has changed our perspective of both the mountain and ourselves. So it is with our view of God. Humility is not making ourselves smaller, but comparing ourselves with something — Someone — bigger.

Humbling oneself is not some magnanimous personal sacrifice. It is nothing more than simply acknowledging reality. The truth is that each person is an ordinary sinner like everyone else. But it is also true that some are sinners who have been saved by God's amazing grace. P. T. Forsyth wrote, "Our churches are full of the nicest, kindest people who have never known the despair of guilt or the breathless wonder of forgiveness."[5] Is it surprising that we have such a struggle with humility? We must return daily to the mirror of the Scriptures and take a long, honest look at ourselves (James 1:21–27).

The first issue we must address is one of honesty. The second is one of *authority*. Who is really in control of our lives? It is easy for us to say that God is in control and that Jesus is Lord, but aside from a specific and decisive transfer of control, we remain the ruler of our lives. It takes more than simply agreeing and believing; it extends beyond the mind and the emotions. We have a chronic need to do what Jesus described as "denying himself" (Luke 9:23). Each day, we must confront the issue of authority in our life and say "no" to self. There needs to be a daily raising of the white flag, a voluntary surrender of ourselves to the King. Surrender of the will is an essential element of intimacy with God.

Saying "no" to self only has muscle as we say "yes" to God. Galatians 5:13–26 puts it in terms of moving from selfishness to Spiritishness.[6] As an intentional, progressive transfer of control, we order our lives according to Spiritish insight rather than selfish impulse. Paul wrote, "Walk by the Spirit, and you will not carry out the desire of the flesh [self]" (Galatians 5:16).

As we repeatedly accept the reality of who we are and surrender to the authority of the Master, we must make ongoing, conscious decisions to animate these spiritual realities. We must *choose to be a servant*, which is not merely choosing to serve. Pride can still rule in choosing to serve. We can selfishly decide when and where we will serve. We can control whom we serve and for how long. We can select an area of service that makes us look good, some area where our strengths will be put on display. We can pick a manner of serving that feeds our ego with the praise and admiration of others.

Choosing to be a servant is very different. In taking this route, we give up all rights, honors, and privileges (Philippians 2:3–8). We make ourselves available to the Master and recognize his right to determine the *whens* and *wheres* of our service. We give Jesus the right to decide whom we will serve and what form that service will take. Choosing to be a servant is a deliberate downsizing of our egos. It is a tangible way of acknowledging that life is not about our own selves.

The Bad News Is the Good News

An amazingly practical value emerges out of this attitude of modesty: it sets us free from pretending that we don't have flaws in our personality. It eliminates that compulsion to hide our weaknesses or excuse the failures that accompany them. Humility releases us from the wearying work of defending our fragile egos. The more we grasp the liberating truth of who we are in Christ, the more we discover that we have nothing to prove and nothing to lose. And with this, we find an increasing freedom to admit mistakes and failures. There is even a possibility of laughing at ourselves. Putting life into truer proportions allows us to see the humor in much of life, as well as in our own quirky behavior.

In other words, humility sets us free to really enjoy life. We no longer have our energy siphoned into an endless pursuit of the meaningless. It gets us out of that continuous jostling for some position in life and eliminates the desperate search for a sense of significance. I once heard someone say that we spend our lives working at jobs we don't enjoy, to make money we don't need, to buy things we don't want, to impress people we don't even like. What an exhausting and futile existence. But as we nurture intimacy with God, we no longer feel the need to create an impressive appearance. It becomes more than enough to simply be who we are in Christ: an ordinary sinner, saved by grace.

Another practical value of humility is that it makes the lessons of life less painful. All of us are guaranteed a cavalcade of personal failures in this life, but humility can reduce the number of those "falls" by lowering our personal center of gravity.

Years ago, when our children were still child-size, my family visited an ice-skating rink located in the middle of a huge shopping mall. Several factors played into this event. I had never skated on ice before, it was lunch time, and there was a class in session for small children. In this mall, it was common for shoppers to eat their lunch while sitting in the mezzanine that surrounded the ice rink. Until I showed up, there wasn't much to watch. Several groups of kids were meandering around the rink in an ice-skating version of follow-the-leader. Each child maintained balance by holding onto a bright orange construction cone, the kind used to merge traffic into one lane while workers take a coffee break. It was a great idea, and because there were a few extra cones around, my children latched onto some of them and away they went. It seemed that everyone had a cone but me. As a result, I became the midday entertainment for the fast-food lunch-bunch while I creatively searched for new ways to splatter myself on the ice. Finally, one of the instructors took pity on me and offered some help. As I joked about my awkwardness on the ice, she consoled me by saying, "Children are not as prone to fall because they have such a low center of gravity. You, on the other hand, . . . "

Keeping a low center of gravity does not prevent us from falling, but it does reduce the frequency of those crashes. And when we do fall (which we will), it's not as far down. Those two concepts, working together, add up to one very appealing outcome — less pain.

One more value of humility is in the area of our practical ability to negotiate life. Like everyone else, I have my strengths and my weaknesses. Where my personal strengths are allowed to flourish, I find that life works well for me. Knowing this, I tend to adjust my life so that it caters to these stronger qualities. But I have also discovered that in these areas of *personal* strength, I experience the least of *God's* strength. There is a logical explanation for this. In these areas, I have a significant degree of self-confidence, and as a result, I don't feel the need to call upon God. While my personal assets are tremendous ego builders, they can actually become liabilities in my walk with Christ and impede my spiritual progress.

Humility is the dynamic that frees us to experience more power in our lives. Only in the acknowledgment of our weaknesses do we open ourselves to the expression of God's power. We must consciously take off our red capes and remove the big "S" from our chest. Paul was so convinced of this that he boldly announced, "I will . . . boast about my weaknesses, so that the power of Christ may dwell in me" (2 Corinthians 12:9). The apostle knew, from personal experience, that the humble are the ones best acquainted with the power of God.

What Did Humility Look Like in Jesus?

I have found only one self-portrait of Jesus in the Scriptures, only one recorded statement in which Jesus describes himself. In Matthew 11:29, Jesus reveals himself as "gentle and humble in heart." Jesus modeled a form of humility that seems foreign to most of the trite definitions I have heard. He brought life and color and power to the term.

Jesus' version was calm but not quiet, confident but without a trace of arrogance. His humility set him free to laugh and enjoy life. He could lavish attention upon others without draining his own self-esteem. He could absorb all sorts of abuse from every imaginable source without becoming bitter or despairing. Humility robbed Jesus' enemies of their targets. And humility made Jesus approachable. The protective barriers that keep others at a safe distance were not a part of his life. Jesus made no attempt to hide anything and exerted no effort to flaunt anything. He was not self-conscious.

It must have been refreshing to be around Jesus. He made no attempts to impress anyone. There was no boasting, no arrogance, no demands that he be the center of attention. He was never defensive or protective of some personal rights. He was never offended by careless comments or social snubs. People didn't have to be cautious with what they said around him, fearing that he might misinterpret their words or misunderstand their intent. He wasn't intimidated by the big shots or embarrassed by the little shots. Jesus was completely at ease whether in the home of a respected community leader, surrounded by successful business owners, or in the home of a notorious swindler, surrounded by prostitutes and criminals. He was free to tell stories to children or touch a leprous man or wash the feet of a Galilean. He had nothing to prove and nothing to lose and everything to teach us:

> Have this attitude in yourselves which was also in Christ Jesus, who, although He existed in the form of God, did not regard equality with God a thing to be grasped, but emptied Himself, taking the form of a bond-servant. (Philippians 2:5–7)

What Does Humility Look Like in Those Close to Jesus?

Humility, as a virtue, does not stifle the pluck and moxie in one's personality. It stands apart from any caricature of a slow-moving, quiet individual with no fire for life and no passion for adventure. Humility is not synonymous with passivity. Jesus didn't set aside his humility while trashing the temple "business district" or while debating the intellectual elite. He didn't compromise his humility by allowing others to serve him or by teaching with authority. So, what *does* humility look like in the life of one who is building intimacy with the Savior? What are the observable characteristics of a humble spirit? The Scriptures call attention to at least three highly visible marks of biblical humility. They are a calm spirit, a teachable attitude, and a servant lifestyle.

A Calm Spirit

A genuinely calm spirit signals a genuinely humble heart. As we encounter obnoxious people, meaningless delays, and things that break or don't work right — as we come up against all of the typical frustrations of life — what happens inside us? Are we frustrated, worried, or intimidated by what we cannot control? How do we respond when our world is shaken by the traumatic or invaded by the unexpected?

As we move closer to Christ, we should find it easier to relinquish control of our life to the Master. The proof that we are doing this shows up as we make fewer demands upon God, fewer demands upon those around us, fewer demands upon life itself. There is a change in the terms, tones, and tactics of our prayers and our conversations. We become much easier to live with. The freedom humility affords us is something we can pass on to those around us.

The calm spirit of humility can be seen in an increasing willingness to wait, slow down, or change direction. When we see life from the vantage point of the lowly, our own schedule is no longer paramount. Someone else has authority over the events of our day, and our response to those events reveals the condition of our relationship with that Someone. Francis Schaeffer wrote, "A quiet disposition and a heart giving thanks at any given moment is the real test of the extent to which we love God at that moment."[7]

A calm spirit is directly related to the posture humility takes in an intimate relationship with God. By its very nature, drawing close to God draws us to our knees. As we bring the trauma and turmoil of our life before God in prayer, as we admit that we are powerless to deal with many of the issues pursuing us through this life, as we take our eyes off of our concerns and bow our head before our awesome God, we discover that we are positioned perfectly to deal with life.

Consider the South African oryx, a variety of antelope known as the "lion killer." The oryx is not a particularly vicious-looking beast. It is about the size of a deer, standing about four feet tall at the shoulder. It is not armed with powerful jaws or razor-sharp claws. In fact, its only defense is a couple of straight, sharp horns that are as long as the animal is tall. The horns appear to be useless since they are pointed directly backward.

When threatened, this antelope's first instinct is to run or to seek the safety of the herd. If the animal is cut off from the others and chased to a point of exhaustion or cornered with no chance of escape, a fascinating scenario unfolds. The oryx faces its attacker, drops to its knees, and bows its head as if to pray. At that point, two things happen. One is that the oryx can no longer see its enemy. The other is that its resources are now focused directly on the problem. To an attacking lion, somewhat lacking in depth perception, these four-foot lances register only as a couple of bull's-eyes on the head of its dinner. So racing full speed at what appears to be a defeated prey, the lion impales itself on the humble "lion killer's" horns.

Humility frees us to bend our knees and bow our head before we have reached a point of desperate exhaustion. It is a prayer life built on an intimate humility before God that confidently focuses the power of that relationship on the issues of our life. Ultimately, this calm spirit displays itself on the face of its owner. As humility pervades the areas of one's life, any hard expressions of arrogance and pride are softened. Proverbs 6:16–17 teaches that whatever is happening in one's heart is ultimately going to sculpt the contours of the face. Our attitudes, our concerns, our pain, our joy — whatever is going on inside us — will make its presence known by the set of our face.

A Teachable Attitude

Next to a calm spirit, one of the most revealing marks of a lowly lifestyle is teachability. The willingness to place oneself under the authority of another is not native to our rebellious spirit. The maturing of humility increases one's receptivity to instruction and correction from others, even from unlikely or undesirable sources.

A biblical writer by the name of James tells us that humility is the key to absorbing God's Word (1:21). Plainly stated, there are to be no barriers or conditions put in the path of God's Word, no excuses or explanations concocted to deflect the impact of the Scriptures. In observable terms, humbly receiving the Word includes such things as listening without defending or justifying oneself. It is asking questions that expose our weaknesses and reveal what we don't know, while refusing to flaunt what we do know (or think we know). While we may not like what we hear or agree with what is said, humility shows up in our willingness not to dominate conversations with our opinions. It frees us to hear unrefined insights without making any adjustments to them. We don't need to have the final word.

Receiving the Word in genuine humility means that we are allowing the truth to find its mark within us. It means that we not only listen to God's Word and respond graciously to God's messenger, but that we also allow ourselves to become vulnerable and pliable. We permit ourselves to be affected emotionally as well as intellectually and grant ourselves every opportunity for the changes of spiritual growth to occur within us. The authenticity of humility can be measured by the consistency of this growth process.

God's plan for spiritual growth in us is not purely academic. God desires a visible, progressive evidence of his life in us, something Scripture describes as spiritual fruit. Our English word "humility" comes from the Latin term *humus*, meaning "earth." Perhaps there is a clue in that word concerning one of God's most common means of achieving his desire in us.

While traveling through California's Central Valley, I saw groves of young trees planted at a forty-five-degree angle. I would have thought that they had been blown over by some great windstorm if I had not noticed that they were actually tied down in that position. When a horticultural expert was asked about the strange sight, he gave, at no extra charge, some personal insight concerning God's humbling work in my life. He referred to this as "stressing" the trees, saying that it retards nonessential growth and increases fruit production. He elaborated on other forms of intentional stress, such as vigorous pruning, withholding water until the trees wilt, starving them of fertilizer, and allowing general neglect. The miniseminar concluded with this statement: "The stress technique is the oldest recognized method of getting established trees to produce fruit." God graciously stresses our lives by bringing us down to earth and removing that which feeds our pride. How we respond to this intentional stressing reveals how intimately acquainted we are with the hand of the Gardener:

> He disciplines us for our good, so that we may share His holiness. All discipline for the moment seems not to be joyful, but sorrowful; yet to those who have been trained by it, afterwards it yields the peaceful fruit of righteousness. (Hebrews 12:10–11)

A Servant Lifestyle

In addition to a calm spirit and a teachable attitude, humility invariably expresses itself in servanthood. Lowliness is countercultural in the direction it takes. It is always seeking some form of "downward" movement. Speaker and author Bill Hybels uses the catchphrase "downward mobility" to describe this.[8] Serving tends to make us "low-maintenance" people. As such, we are not draining the time, energy, and patience of others. We are "putting in" more than we are "taking out" of any situation. Humbly serving others reverses the arrogant assumption within us that others are on earth to meet our needs. We become more of a "dog" person (remember Roscoe?).

As the leveling process works itself out in one's life, it creates a freedom to turn attention away from oneself and direct it toward others. Increasingly, conversations can be filled with questions that show interest in someone other than one's own self. If we are acting in humility, we will be seeking very practical ways of making those around us feel significant. It is a tangible form of "looking out for the interests of others" (Philippians 2:3–4). There should be a growing awareness of the needs around us and visible evidence that we are willingly directing our time and resources toward meeting them. Humility frees us to invest our life in others without feeling that we are on the losing end of the deal.

Lunch with Jesus

Missionary and author Elisabeth Elliot concludes her book *These Strange Ashes* by relating a fictional tale (to which I have given my own twist) of Jesus and his disciples. The story takes place on a day when Jesus was teaching some of those essential lessons of life to his core of twelve. On this particular day, Jesus stopped along a path and instructed the disciples to each pick up a stone and carry it for him. They all complied, selecting stones of various sizes. Peter, not wanting to overdo things, chose one that would not be too much of a burden, more in the range of a pebble than a stone.

They traveled to the top of a mountain, and there Jesus turned the stones into bread. Tired and very hungry, they each had food proportionate to what they had chosen to carry for the Master. Peter would have had nothing more than a cracker for lunch that day, but John gave him some of his.

It was about a week later that Jesus repeated his stone-carrying instructions to his band of future leaders. Now Peter was not about to make the same mistake twice, so he heaved upon his shoulder the largest rock he could find. He was going to eat well that day.

Jesus led them down along shaded banks of the Jordan River, looking for just the right place to stop. When he found it, he simply told them to throw their stones into the river. As Peter's rock dropped from his shoulder, he stared at the Master in disbelief. Jesus met his gaze, came close to the hungry disciple, and whispered these words, "For whom did you carry the stone?"[9]

It is so easy to get things turned around. We can easily find ourselves serving for our own benefit. Intimate humility keeps before each one of us the question, "For whom am I carrying the stone?"

Conclusion

One of the most freeing qualities of the Christian life is humility. It is freedom from oneself. It is freedom to see things the way they really are. It is freedom to grow and change and enjoy what God is doing. Humility keeps us from tripping over our own "self." The maturing qualities of biblical humility are the natural consequences of moving ever closer to the awesome God of the Scriptures. Increasing evidence of a calm spirit, a teachable attitude, and a servant lifestyle marks the reality of spiritual intimacy in our life.

The issues of honesty and authority are never fully laid to rest. Our selfish nature, or the "flesh" as it is called in the Scriptures, is always finding creative new platforms for expression. But as we move closer to God, we become progressively more aware of the majesty of his greatness and of our relative insignificance. At the same time, we recognize more clearly God's goodness and provision for us and find ourselves increasingly wrapped up in Yahweh instead of ourselves. We come to grips with the fact that we are not *the* God. We are not *a* god. We are not even a god-ette. As we watch the Awesome One at work in our lives, we find ourselves increasingly amazed, saying "God loves me and cares for my every need. He, alone, is God."

Drawing Closer

1. In what specific ways do you see yourself living a self-hyphenated life? What do these reveal about your relationship with God?

2. How has authentic biblical humility expressed itself in your life over the past month? How has this humility been a direct result of intimacy with God?

3. What is your reaction to the quotation from P. T. Forsyth on page 125? How does it relate to you?

4. How would a greater development of biblical humility set you free to enjoy life more than you do today?

5. In what ways does your life match Peter's in the "stone" story? How would you respond to the question Jesus asked of Peter?

——෨ TEN ෨——

Serious Laughter

(putting a different spin on life's circumstances)

A S A YOUNG PASTOR, I ATTENDED A CONFERENCE IN WHICH I FOUND myself focusing more on the personalities of the main speakers than on the content of their presentations. I discovered that the trait I most envied in these people was their ability to enjoy life. They appeared to have complete freedom to laugh loudly and genuinely and to absorb enthusiastically all that was going on around them. I have come to prize such people as refreshing models for my own life.

Over the years, it has been distressing for me to discover how many believers consider such genuine happiness a luxury in this life. It is far too easy to retreat into a sullen lifestyle, viewing Christianity as meaningful but not necessarily happy. But the abundant life to which Jesus Christ has called us cannot be confined to simply a "meaningful" life. It also demands the unrestricted delight of living out that meaning, a delight whose silent absence never goes unnoticed.

Joy is one of the greatest attractions to the Christian life. It is also one of the most profound marks of intimacy with God. Joy is the emotional charge that comes with our new life in Christ. As part of being "fully alive," God intends for his people to have their emotional lives clicked on.

Joy is an appropriate response to good news. If good news is legitimate and if we have some understanding of its implications, our emotions kick in. When a cancer victim receives news that she has gone into remission or a prisoner learns that he is to be released or a waitress discovers that she has won a million dollars or a young man hears that the girl of his dreams will marry him (especially if she is the

135

waitress), something happens inside that lights up the entire person. Such news demands an emotional response. In fact, we would have serious questions about someone who did not show any indications of excitement or delight at hearing these things.

So when we hear that God loves us and has determined not to go through eternity without us, that should stir our emotions. When we find out that God has forgiven our sin and banished every trace of our guilt, that should release a cry of delight. When we discover that God has great dreams for us that exceed our wildest goals for ourselves, that should excite every fiber in our being. All this is genuinely "good" news and demands a response.

Joy is an emotion and an attitude at the same time. As an emotion, it is the feeling we experience when we get our heart's desire. As an attitude, it is the positive mind-set that governs our emotions by anchoring them to the truth of God's Word.

The Emotion of Joy

As an emotion, joy combines the thrill of winning a contest, the an-ticipation of opening a special gift, the delight of meeting a long-lost friend, the amazement of a new discovery, the energy of a celebration, and the pleasure of a quiet evening. There are times when authen-tic joy requires an expression like singing or shouting or dancing — occasions when nothing else is adequate. And other times call for a delight that is best expressed in quiet pleasure. Joy is the ability to recognize the goodness of God and the freedom to respond to it.

Somewhere along the way, joy was robbed of its feeling. Many of the emotionless definitions floating on the tides of Christian thought today seem to make joy a bit numb. Accordingly, it would appear possible to have joy without feeling anything or displaying any overt signs of emotional life. By describing joy as a hidden attitude of the heart that has no emotional connection to our voice or face, we end up with sober, somber Christians who stifle the music of their spiritual life.

Pressing the point even further, I believe it is biblically incorrect to make a radical distinction between joy and happiness. It is not true that happiness is worldly and joy is spiritual. Nor is it true that happiness is some shallow feeling tied to the circumstances of life and that joy is a more mature sensation of well-being that is not determined by the course of events or the state of affairs. The Scriptures never condemn happiness as a worldly emotion. Happiness is never framed as a quality foreign to God's people or incompatible with joy. In fact, joy and happiness are sometimes mentioned in connection with each other, mingling their meanings.[1] Other times, joy is associated with various emotional actions like singing, shouting, or dancing. Joy is something that is felt, not just deep down in some baffled chamber of the heart, but throughout one's entire being. We cannot justify its absence by merely toying with semantics.

The Attitude of Joy

As an attitude, joy is a decision. While we cannot determine our circumstances, we can decide what our attitude will be in the midst of any situation. We can choose to be joyful. That is both liberating and threatening. It is liberating to know that we don't have to be cranky and crabby. Life doesn't have to get us down. The attitude of joy can keep us buoyant while those around us are sinking. Charles Fuller encouraged this attitude when he wrote, "Seek to cultivate, as a plain duty, a joyous sense of the crowded kindnesses of God in your everyday life."

It is, however, threatening to know that much of what we might call being "realistic" is really nothing more than an excuse for being grumpy and negative. We cannot say that we are in a right relationship with God while sporting an "Eeyore" mentality. That is a contradiction in terms. As life presents itself, we choose how we will respond.

Many years ago, my father-in-law, Dr. Roy Kraft, found himself in a social squeeze. He had been invited into a home for dinner. The hostess had prepared a very special evening, including his favorite dessert, custard pie. But when the dessert was served, he noticed that there was an ingredient not usually included in this treat — a fly. There it was, just beneath the glaze on the custard.

Seated next to the hostess, my father-in-law had time only for a quick decision. If he mentioned it to her, she would be mortified. If he scooped it out, she might find it later. And if he sat there staring at the pie much longer, she would begin to wonder what was wrong. He decided it was a matter of attitude. He could choose how he would respond to this "fly in his life." He rationalized that the fly had obviously been cooked enough to kill any deadly diseases. So, with a bit of a crunch not common to custard pie, my father-in-law enjoyed his dessert with a smile and a quick swallow of coffee.

There is always going to be a fly in the pie somewhere. Life is constantly presenting opportunities to make decisions about our attitude. These are decisions to anchor our emotions to the solid rock of God's Word. When it comes right down to it, each of us is the one and only person responsible for our own bad attitudes. We are also responsible for our experience of joy.

How Does Intimacy Produce Joy?

Joy is both provided by God (John 15:11; Galatians 5:22) and demanded by him. The heavenly Father requires that his children be joyful. The command to rejoice is repeated over fifty times in the Scriptures. Failure to develop joy in our relationship with God is to register discontent as a by-product of its neglect.

There are three basic components to igniting and stoking the joy that marks new life in Christ. They are intimacy, anticipation, and expression. To know the joy God intends for us, we must be drawing ever closer to the source of joy, becoming increasingly aware of his goodness in our lives and consciously focusing attention on what we have found.

The Presence of Joy

The joy associated with the Christian life is touched off by the presence of Jesus. The Westminster Catechism states, "The chief end and duty of man is to glorify God and to enjoy Him forever." Psalm 37:4 says, "Delight yourself in the LORD." Psalm 16:11 says,

> In Your presence is fullness of joy;
> In Your right hand there are pleasures forever.

David wrote that such Presence is the ultimate joy. It is the exhilaration of being near one who is truly awesome and majestic and realizing that you belong there. It is the overwhelming pleasure of standing before one who sees right through you and yet grasping the fact that he loves you completely. It is the accelerated heartbeat from venturing close to him and the surprise of being drawn even closer.

Consider this prayer by Robert Moyan:

> Grant unto us, O God, the royalty of inward happiness and the serenity which comes from living close to Thee. Daily renew in us the sense of joy, and let Thy eternal Spirit dwell in our souls and bodies, filling every corner of our hearts with light and Grace, so that, bearing about with the infection of good courage, we may be diffusers of life, and may meet all ills and cross-accidents, even death itself, with gallant and high-hearted happiness, giving Thee thanks always for all things; through Jesus Christ our Lord. Amen.

Drawing closer to God begins by removing the joy inhibitors in our lives. Dealing with the issues that produce guilt, fear, pride, and insecurity is part of the process of developing intimacy. The very things that create distance between God and us are the same things that separate us from the experience of joy. And since God is our joy, whatever obstructs our relationship with Yahweh becomes an obstacle to joy.

As we remove what inhibits joy, we are able to pursue freely what enhances it. Part of what keeps a sense of excitement growing in any relationship is the continuous discovery of new insights into the other person. Exploring the heart and soul of someone is a never-ending adventure. With each discovery, the relationship is refreshed and renewed. It becomes deeper and more complex. The value of the person increases in our own mind. There are new things to cherish. Intimacy deepens. Joy comes in celebrating what we have found.

Once again, the Bible is essential. Psalm 19:8 says that God's Word rejoices the heart. There are several ways to view this joy-producing Book. It can be seen as a textbook, full of facts concerning God's eternal plan and the historical fulfillment of it. The Bible can be viewed as a guidebook, comprising instructions and insights for successful living. But those same pages can also be considered God's love letters to us, intended to let us into his heart and to build our relationship with God. While all of these are true, it is the last of them that brings the greatest potential for joy.

During my first year at Biola University, my bride-to-be was nearly four hundred miles away. We wrote several times each week. I searched my mailbox daily for those letters. When they arrived, I would pore over them, spending most of my time between the lines, longing for the latest assurance that she still loved me. Each time I read of her love for me, I experienced the same rush of excited joy. I believe God wants his words to have that same effect on all of us.

As we open God's Word each day with the intention of discovering something new about him, God delights in revealing the deepest secrets of his heart to us. God does not want us just to know *about* him. God wants us to really *know* him and, in the knowing, to experience the joy of what we find.

The Anticipation of Joy

Joy seems to draw much of its energy from anticipation. As an expression of intimacy, it begins by learning more about who God is, what Yahweh is like, and how he goes about things. Joy grows then as we expectantly watch for God to be and do what he has said. The more we can envision God in the midst of our circumstances, the more excited we become. We are to watch for the evidence of Yahweh's goodness and look for the fingerprints of God on the circumstances of our lives. Remember, we find whatever we go looking for. And what we find reveals what we have sought. Joy comes from having tasted the goodness of God and from knowing that more is coming.

Joy does not exempt one from pain, sorrow, and distress. In fact, those experiences actually play an important role in the anticipation of joy. The intensity of one's pain often determines the intensity of one's joy. The Scriptures are filled with examples of this. A barren woman finally conceives in her old age and gives birth to a son. A leprous man is healed. People who have feared for their lives watch as an attacking army is swallowed up in the Red Sea. Parents receive their daughter back from the dead. In each case, there was definite agony before ecstasy. Imagine the sight of David dancing in the street as the ark of the covenant was brought to Jerusalem. What a picture of unrestrained delight! But the ecstatic moment was preceded by seventy years when the Holy of Holies had an emptiness in its very core. It was the *return* that brought joy.

Eugene Peterson has written, "A common but futile strategy for achieving joy is trying to eliminate things that hurt: get rid of pain by numbing the nerve ends, get rid of insecurity by eliminating risks, get rid of disappointments by depersonalizing your relationships. And then try to lighten the boredom of such a life by buying joy in the form of vacations and entertainment.... Laughter is the result of living in the midst of God's great works."[2]

There are, I believe, no ordinary days in the lives of God's people. There is never an insignificant day when nothing of consequence is going on in the life of a believer, never a day that doesn't matter. God is always at work doing awesome things that count in light of eternity. Regardless of what is going on, there is always something bigger happening. Joy is produced by anticipating God's goodness in unexpected places. It is a matter of giving ourselves the freedom to enjoy what God is doing in our lives, even when we don't understand all (or any) of it. Joy is the result of looking past our problems to a point of blessing. In the midst of a dark period in David's life, the king of ancient Israel wrote,

> I would have despaired unless I had believed that I would see the goodness of the LORD in the land of the living. — Psalm 27:13

The Expression of Joy

God made us in *his* image, and with that came the capacity to smile, laugh, and sing.[3] We are instructed to release the content of our hearts in the form of praise. Joyful praise is not the same as an emotional free-for-all. It is not a frivolous activity intended to whip up our emotions. C. S. Lewis once said, "There is a kind of happiness and wonder that makes you serious."[4] Author Flannery O'Connor captures this same thought: "Where there is no belief in the soul, there is very little drama.... Either one is serious about salvation or one is not. And it is well to realize that the maximum amount of seriousness admits the maximum amount of comedy. Only if we are secure in our beliefs can we see the comical side of the universe."[5]

Ephesians 5:18–19 exhorts us to

Be filled with the Spirit, speaking to one another in psalms and hymns and spiritual songs, singing and making melody with your heart to the Lord.

Joy is a matter of choosing what we will allow our minds to dwell upon. This instruction was so vital to the spiritual health of God's people that Paul stated it twice in one verse. Philippians 4:4 says, "Rejoice in the Lord always; again I will say, rejoice!"

In verse 8, Paul gets very specific about what is to fill our minds. We are to dwell upon those things that are true, honorable, right, pure, lovely, and of good repute. That which has excellence and is worthy of praise should dominate our thinking. That doesn't mean that we pretend there are no problems in the world. But it does mean that we choose not to be driven by negative thinking (which is, by the way, a sound mental-health practice). Proverbs 17:22 confirms this: "A cheerful heart is good medicine" (NIV).

To rejoice is to direct our attention to that which brings us joy. If we find our joy in money, then thinking about money will make us feel good. If we find our joy in sports or shopping or in a certain person, then focusing our minds on such things will lift our spirits and make us feel good — in other words, joyful. The problem is that all these things don't address what we truly desire — those deepest longings within us. Biblical joy is not simply a personality trait; it is a supernatural quality. The difference is in the source of the joy.

The Bible tells us that our deepest longings cannot be satisfied by anything in this world. Every day, millions of people rediscover a common reality. They are faced with the fact that all the power and possessions they can accumulate, all the sex and entertainment they can experience, and all the drugs and alcohol they can consume will never satisfy the legitimate cravings of the heart. Only God can do that. The overwhelming joy of a relationship with Christ is captured in 1 Peter 1:8: "You greatly rejoice with joy inexpressible." Psalm 43:4 says,

> I will go to the altar of God,
> To God my exceeding joy.

When we call attention to what God has done through words that are spoken or sung, we confirm the reality of God's goodness in our own mind. We confound the negative self-talk that tends to overwhelm our thinking. Rejoicing is an intentional altering of our attitude. When we praise the goodness of God, we force ourselves to acknowledge something our selfish heart chooses to resist. When we sing that praise, we command our emotions to celebrate Yahweh's goodness.

What Does Joy Look Like?

In general terms, joy becomes visible in the sheer pleasure of living. We become more proficient at recognizing the goodness of God in the events of our life. As we give ourselves the freedom to respond to that goodness, we become more pleasant to be around. In other words, life becomes less and less of a hassle or a drudgery. There is an increasing expectation of surprises from God. An inner strength emerges from a joyful heart and is revealed in confident responses to circumstances. The more this increases, the less we will appear to be threatened by life. We discover what the Bible means when it says, "The joy of the LORD is your strength" (Nehemiah 8:10).

Nehemiah 8 tells of a priest by the name of Ezra who had just read a portion of God's Word to those in rebuilt Jerusalem who had returned from captivity in Babylon. Having heard the Scriptures, the people were first struck by the spiritual failures of their past and the utter shambles of their present lives before God. The guilt and despair over their weakness produced a visible and very appropriate grief to which Ezra applied the words, "The joy of the LORD is your strength."

The impact of having been set free from our old life is powerful. This is true for everyone, no matter who they are, no matter how old or how much wreckage they leave behind. Joy is visible in the upbeat confidence of that freedom. It puts a genuinely positive spin on life that can be seen specifically in our facial and vocal expressions.

Facial Expression

Joy is also an easy mark of spiritual life to identify. It is literally written all over one's face. Proverbs 15:13 says, "A joyful heart makes a cheerful face."

If we claim to know the joy of the Lord, it should be evident somehow on our face. This does not mean that we must walk around with a goofy grin or a plastic smile, but it does mean that if the landscape of our face is always hard and frequently formed into frowns or expressions of anger, something is dreadfully wrong within us. One's face exposes one's heart. A cheerful face is one that is animated by the life within. It is in the process of developing "smile lines." Over the years, the contours of one's face should progressively reveal the shape of one's heart. A simple reality check can be performed in front of a mirror. Ask yourself what your face says about the joy you claim to possess in Christ.

While the world around us attempts to look confident and unmoved by circumstances, its face often betrays a sense of lifeless existence. Many appear bored with life, disinterested by design. In the midst of that, our faces should present a contrast. The fact that we are loved and forgiven should soften the default settings of our countenance. The latest evidence of God's goodness should put a conspicuous glint in our eyes. Life for God's people is anything but boring, and our faces should advertise that reality. Besides, the Bible says, this emotional "life" looks good on God's people (Psalm 33:1).

Vocal Expression

Not only does our heart show up on our face, it spills out of our mouth. No matter how hard we work at gracious speech, emphasizing courtesy, respect, and the latest in politically correct terminology, the condition of our heart will find a way into our conversation. But recognizing God's goodness in our life and in the affairs that swirl around us makes an impact on our thinking and on how we feel about life. Our pessimistic commentary on life is gradually edited from our conversation, replaced by encouraging words with a positive twist.

Connectedness to God can be measured, to some extent, in decibels. Where once there was silence, now there are songs. As our love relationship with God grows, there is a corresponding need and desire to express that love with passion. Singing allows words to take on more intensity. With the passing of time, there should be an expanding repertoire of songs. Some of them will take us back to significant points in our spiritual journey, and others will capture the vitality of our present walk with the Savior. Some songs will connect us to our spiritual heritage or to some great truth of the Scriptures, while others will allow us inside the hearts of other believers. Sometimes words alone are not enough to express the joy of our life in Christ. The words search for some emotional means of being expressed. They grope for songs.

God has determined that the power of his kingdom shall be wrapped in the songs of his saints. I can assure you that this is not a matter of having a good voice. I am one of those who seems to have a design flaw in the sound department. In fact, one of the things I look forward to as standard equipment in my heavenly body is the ability to sing with perfect pitch from a perfect heart.

One aspect of joy goes beyond the ability of words and songs to express. It simply comes out in laughter. Psalm 126:2 describes the emotions of those Jews who returned from the Babylonian Captivity:

> Then our mouth was filled with laughter,
> And our tongue with joyful shouting.

Job 8:19–21 makes this announcement:

> "This is the joy of His way; . . .
> "He will yet fill your mouth with laughter,
> And your lips with shouting."

I once had the privilege of speaking to a small band of Russian heroes who had lived through the dark oppression of the Soviet system. We met in a hollow gray house in the Siberian city of Novosibirsk. I tried to encourage these believers and made some rather unimpressive (and unsuccessful) attempts to draw laughter from them. After the meeting, one of the older believers helped me gain some perspective. "You must understand that for us, it seems that life was meant to be endured, not enjoyed," he said. But then he added, "Maybe one day we will learn to laugh." The "enduring" of life can leach the joy out of the Christian experience.

Several years later, on a mission trip to Cebu, I stayed up late one evening in the sweltering heat to talk over "old times" with several friends. We sat around a large oak dining table and gabbed about some of the adventures we had experienced together on previous trips to other parts of the world. Although there had been considerable danger involved in those exploits, they took on humorous features as we reminisced. The more we talked, the more we laughed. We laughed until we hurt, until there were tears in our eyes and we were literally sliding out of our chairs. It became a full-fledged endorphin frenzy. The laughter was so loud and prolonged that other members of the team began to make their way out of their rooms to find out what was going on. They found places around the table and stared curiously at their spiritual leaders delirious with laughter.

Ah, it feels so good to laugh! When was the last time you laughed so hard you cried? I am not talking about laughing at twisted jokes or contrived comedy routines. There is, instead, a kind of laughter that comes from seeing the foibles of life for what they are. It is an emotional release that surges forth when we don't make every detail of life a serious issue. God says it's good for one's soul to laugh (Proverbs 17:22). I have learned that is true. Joy releases its energy in bursts of laughter, not because life is funny, but because new life is so fantastic. It is like a child's squeal of delight that cannot be contained.

"I am all in favor of laughing," wrote G. K. Chesterton. "Laughter has something in it in common with the ancient winds of faith and inspiration; it unfreezes pride and unwinds secrecy; it makes men forget themselves in the presence of something greater than themselves; something they cannot resist."[6]

Humor-Impaired?

Did you know that there is no record of Jesus ever laughing or smiling and only one reference to him singing? I found that to be a disturbing discovery, particularly because my mental picture of Jesus has him smiling and singing and laughing often. Jesus attended parties and weddings. He was frequently a guest in homes. I have a hard time believing that he was humor-impaired in those situations and that his only words were statements of deep truth, uttered with serious finality.

I don't believe that Jesus introduced his open-air seminars with a few jokes (although he could have). I cannot quite picture him starting out with lines like, "Hey, did you hear the one about the

Pharisee who . . . ?" I don't think Jesus ever had to add the "just kidding" disclaimer to any of his statements. Jesus did not set out to be funny or amusing. His message was deadly serious.

But there had to be times when Jesus sat around a fire with his friends talking about life. As they did, I wonder if they ever began laughing and continued to laugh until they cried. I wonder how often those friends sang together, aside from the designated singalong times. I wonder if Jesus laughed at Matthew's jokes. Surely he had a few. I wonder why children approached Jesus so readily. Could it have been his smile and the joyful tone of his voice? Can you picture Jesus ever being crabby or expressing a bad attitude with a long, audible sigh? I can't.

Conclusion

Joy is not simply a "Christian" word. Anyone can be joyful. Transforming the naturally joyful into the biblically joyful is a matter of changing the source of one's pleasure. It is the growing ability to recognize the goodness of God and the increasing freedom to respond to it.

Joy is to be the norm, not the exception, in a believer (John 15:11; Galatians 5:22). This in no way diminishes the validity of the emotional battles within each of us (2 Corinthians 1:8). There are appropriate times for tears and mourning (Ecclesiastes 3:4), but the relentless buoyancy of the Christian life always prevails:

> Weeping may last for the night,
> But a shout of joy comes in the morning.
> — Psalm 30:5

In her book *The Courage to Be Happy*, Dorothy Thompson comments on a phrase used by Joseph Joubert, a French writer during the Napoleonic era, in a letter to his beloved Pauline de Beaumont. "One must learn to love life," he insisted. "I cannot admire you as I would wish until I perceive in you the most beautiful of all forms of courage, the courage to be happy." Dorothy Thompson then admits, "Never before had it occurred to me that it required courage to be happy, or that happiness is a demonstration of courage. Courage had always seemed ... the spirit that bravely endured *un* happiness."[7]

It is easy to breed self-pity. It is easy to become consumed with pessimism and anger at the world. There will always be plenty of opportunities to "cash in" on painful experiences. It is so very easy to conclude that new life in Christ is meaningful but not necessarily happy. It may be that one of the most courageous advances you make in your walk with the Master is a venture into the genuine pleasure of God's company.

Drawing Closer

1. Describe three ways you have seen God's goodness in your life over the past week. At what point did you recognize this goodness, and how did you respond to it?

2. How do you see your experience of joy changing as you move closer to God? How might others describe these changes in you?

3. In what ways do you allow your emotions to drive your relationship with God? What is one specific action you can take to turn this around?

4. When do you "feel" the closest to God? Describe how that feels. How does joy factor into your description?

5. What is your interpretation of Joseph Joubert's phrase "the courage to be happy"? How does it relate to your connectedness to God?

ᏻ ELEVEN ᏻ

More Than Words

(overcoming life's obstacles)

I FIRST BECAME ACQUAINTED WITH THE CONCEPT OF ANAEROBIC exercise at a personal level while mountain biking with my son. We were in the coastal mountains north of Santa Cruz, California. On this particular trail, there were plenty of long, tedious climbs and wild "Mad Hatter" descents. There were also spectacular views of the Pacific Ocean, as we alternately passed through groves of oaks and redwoods. Some of the uphill portions of the trek were more of a challenge for me than for my son. Torquing the pedals on those steeper hills, I found my energy quickly depleted. I went beyond just being out of breath and physically tired. My lungs burned, my legs ached, and my head throbbed (fun, huh?). I would push myself as far as I could go but would fall far short of making it to the crest. Having reached a state of exhaustion, I found even walking the remaining distance to be a test. When I finally made it, I was ready to collapse. I had gone beyond the limits of my physical resources. It was an anaerobic experience.

An "anaerobic" lifestyle, one in which we live beyond our inner resources, seems fairly common today. So are the physical and emotional collapses that accompany such a practice. It is surprising how quickly our personal strength is consumed, no matter how strong we think we are. It sure seems like there are a lot of hills to climb. Second Corinthians 4:8–9 identifies four of those hills that drain personal strength, four experiences that are common to everyone. It says that we are afflicted, perplexed, persecuted, and struck down. Yep, those will do it!

We are *afflicted*. This refers to the normal irritations, annoyances, and pressures of life. Affliction is composed of long lines and deadlines, unexpected bills and inflexible schedules, things that don't work right and people that don't work right. Affliction includes those undesirable, pressurized responsibilities of relationships and occupations and personal goals. Affliction cranks up the stress level and wipes out our emotional reserves.

I saw an element of this played out while browsing in a shop one day. I overheard a telephone conversation between a clerk and an irate customer. She spoke graciously and chose her words carefully, but her voice carried throughout the store. It was obvious that the person on the other end was making unreasonable demands and punctuating them with colorful language. After about ten minutes of getting nowhere, the exasperated clerk tactfully suggested, "Let me check with my manager." With that, she put the call on hold, screamed, and beat the telephone receiver on the counter. Then, composing herself and running her fingers playfully through her hair, she returned to her conversation with a calm voice.

There are times (perhaps many of them) when we would love to put life on hold for a few moments so that we could scream and smack something on a hard surface. I am no exception. We all need something inside that calms our spirit and keeps us from expending energy on adrenalized responses to annoyances. We need something to counterbalance the pressures of life. Without some kind of substantial personal infrastructure, the intensity of affliction can be crushing.

We are *perplexed*. Life is filled with so many frustrating questions that can't be answered. There are random pieces of life that don't seem to fit together and certain events that don't appear to make any sense at all. We are forced to make tough decisions, and we feel inadequate to face them. Life can become so complicated and confusing. We are people searching for answers that God has chosen to withhold, surrounded by others who are equally perplexed.

We need something to get us through those times when there are no answers, when we can't sort it all out and make sense of life. We need something within us that calms the fear of the unexplainable, something that allows us to be at ease with what is incomplete. We need something solid in our innermost being that keeps us from being deflated by the absence of an answer, something to keep us from despair.

We are *persecuted*. Life isn't fair. No one is exempt from painful experiences. We all go through some degree of physical, mental, and emotional abuse. It is not difficult to think of times when we have been treated unfairly or criticized unjustly. Deliberate snubs and malicious attacks are part of everyone's life story. Somehow, those events tend to become lodged in our permanent memory banks.

At least some of the unkind actions of others have been provoked and are deserved as natural consequences of our own behavior. Other actions that we may consider mistreatment are nothing more than our own misunderstandings and misinterpretations of what is going on. But even after we account for those possibilities, there are still some very real and very painful persecutions.

I have listened to the nightmarish stories of Russian believers who endured the political persecution of the Communist years. The brutal beatings, the late-night searches by police, the imprisonments, and the agonizing loss of loved ones — it was all beyond belief. But one doesn't have to live in some foreign country to experience the reality of persecution. I have also heard far too many accounts of family feuds and domestic violence, of innocent people finding themselves the target of personal attacks and legal vendettas.

Persecution leaches the vitality from our self-worth, leaving us feeling abandoned and rejected. We need an undetachable power source that continuously reinforces our value. We need perpetual reassurance that a presence bigger than ourself is committed to us and supporting us. We need the power to forgive and the ability to move past the painful experiences of life.

We are *struck down*. Life involves catastrophes and shattering blows. A loved one dies. A home goes up in flames. Cancer is diagnosed. Divorce papers arrive. A financial disaster strikes. These calamities tend to arrive abruptly, announced with a siren, a phone call, a letter. Such events are usually cold, indiscriminate, and violent. These are times when life knocks you over; you are "struck down."

I have heard that there is no pain on earth more intense than that which accompanies the loss of a child. Recently, in the space of a week, I have sat beside two mothers who were each going through

that excruciating pain. Both of these women were well-seasoned believers who had successfully raised large families. Each of them had
poured themselves into their children, sacrificing personal interests
for the sake of their children. Neither of these mothers ever dreamed
that she would outlive her offspring. In each case, the death was
sudden and unexpected. The news assaulted their fragile hearts with
a force that threatened to destroy them. They were "struck down."

Such experiences are graphic reminders that we need something to
take us through the toughest times of life. We need something more
than a philosophy or a support group. It's not professional counseling
or financial aid that will make the difference. We need something
that will withstand the devastating blows of a hostile environment.

Beyond Our Ability

The Bible uses ten different words to capture variations on the theme
of power. Five Hebrew words in the Old Testament and five Greek
ones in the New Testament can all be translated "power." These
words express energy and action, strength and might, confirming
the fact that power is woven into the very fabric of God's kingdom: "the kingdom of God does not consist in words, but in power"
(1 Corinthians 4:20).

Power is an unmistakable mark of one who both knows God personally and who is growing in that relationship with Yahweh. This
power is not something that God gives to us as some sort of spiritual commodity, but we receive power as God's spirit actually invades
our lives. God gives power by giving himself. Consider the following
portions of God's Word:

> You shall receive power when the Holy Spirit has come upon you.
> (Acts 1:8)

> For this reason, I bow my knees before the Father, ... that He would grant
> you ... to be strengthened with power through His Spirit in the inner man.
> (Ephesians 3:14–16)

In the New Testament, most of the references to power use a word
referring to "potential" power. In other words, it is an energy that is
real and legitimate but only as a possibility. It is a force that is not

yet realized and of which there is little or no observable evidence. The moment one receives Jesus as Savior, that person receives unlimited potential power. God calls us to turn that latent potential into applied potential.

Spiritual power can be divided into two categories: the access to change and the ability to overcome. As the access to change, spiritual power actuates the Scriptures in one's life. The personal changes that were previously out of reach, inaccessible, are now within grasp. We can actually become a living fulfillment of God's Word. We can deal decisively with the destructive habits and addictions in our lives. We can live the reality of 2 Corinthians 5:17:

> Therefore if any man is in Christ, he is a new creature; the old things passed away; behold, new things have come.

As the ability to overcome, spiritual power equips us with an inner force that allows us to address the obstacles of life. We can face the pressures, the setbacks, the struggles, the challenges, and all the painful realities that are part of the drama of life. We attach ourselves to biblical promises, not for the hope of escaping these realities, but for the legitimate confidence of going through them without being crushed. Isaiah 40:29 says,

> He gives strength to the weary,
> And to him who lacks might
> He increases power.

The Power of Spiritual Intimacy

There are three basic steps to realizing the power of spiritual intimacy in life. First, we must acknowledge our own weakness. Second, we must place ourselves under the authority of God's Word. And third, we must be proactive in prayer.

Intimate Confession

In order to experience God's power in life, we must first stop relying upon our own. This is perhaps the most difficult aspect of spiritual power. It goes back to dealing with all of those self-hyphenated terms

in chapter 9. Personal efforts in the form of self-determination, discipline, aggressiveness, and positive thinking do not enhance God's
work in our life but distract from it:

> He has said to me, "My grace is sufficient for you, for power is perfected
> in weakness." Most gladly, therefore, I will rather boast about my weak-
> nesses, that the power of Christ may dwell in me. Therefore I am well
> content with weaknesses, with insults, with distresses, with persecutions,
> with difficulties, for Christ's sake; for when I am weak, then I am strong.
> (2 Corinthians 12:9–10)

God's intention is to put his life (and power) on display in us.
In any area of our life where we appear strong or self-reliant, God's
presence is obscured. We get in the way. We become the center of
attention, not God. In order for spiritual power to be made visible,
God does not want us to *become* weak but simply to admit our fragile,
powerless nature.

The concept is simple. Until we are willing to be honest with
ourselves and agree that we are powerless to deal effectively with the
issues in life, we will not look to God for power. God is not arbitrating
a fifty-fifty deal (or any other percentage) with us. Either we look to
ourselves for the strength to cope with life, or we look to Yahweh. It
is a choice that is made and remade throughout each day of our lives.

In 1343, a ten-year-old boy became duke of what is now Belgium.
He was Raynald III. Self-absorbed, emotionally unstable, and always
in trouble, Raynald was a slave to his own passions. He was em-
barrassingly obese, and the general population scornfully nicknamed
him Crassus, which means "fat."

Raynald and his younger brother, Edward, quarreled often. As
young men, their conflict took the form of heading opposing political
parties and ultimately led to open battle. Edward, the more "warlike
and aggressive," defeated his brother and had him imprisoned in
Nieuwkerk Castle. In order to avoid any charges of cruelty, Edward
put Raynald in a room with no bars on the windows and no locks
on the doors. Instead, Edward simply had the openings narrowed to
a size that only a slender frame could pass through. Edward could
honestly say, "My brother is not a prisoner. He may leave when he
so wills."

Knowing his brother's weakness, Edward kept a continuous supply of delicious food coming to the cell. For the next ten years, Crassus was willing to forfeit his freedom in order to feed his appetite. He became fatter and more pitiful as the years went by. Finally, Edward was killed in battle, and Raynald was released. But during those years his health had deteriorated along with what little ability he had to rule. He died within a year.[1]

Relying on our own strength leaves us a slave to our own passions. We find ourselves forfeiting our freedom in order to feed our destructive appetites. Until we are willing to admit we have such weaknesses and look away from ourselves to the one who can give the strength to overcome the self, freedom remains only a possibility, not a reality.

This type of personal confession does not occur in surface relationships. Our weaknesses are usually well-defended, being unacceptable subjects for conversation. For many, there is virtually no one on the face of this earth to whom they would admit honestly their fears and frailties. There is no one close enough to be trusted with such sensitive information. The degree to which we are willing to admit our weakness to God determines the extent of the power we can experience in life. This true confession is directly proportionate to the closeness we have cultivated with God.

Intimate Confidence

The second step is to place ourselves under the authority of God's Word. Spiritual power is inseparably tied to God's Word (Romans 1:16; 1 Corinthians 1:18; 2 Peter 1:3–4). When Jesus went through his temptation experience in the desert, he quoted Scripture at each point of attack. In doing so, he was not casting some magic spell from his spiritual handbook; instead he was announcing the authority under which he was acting. By aligning his life with Scriptures, Jesus was tapping into a power source.

Jesus was once approached by a Roman centurion and asked to heal the soldier's servant (Matthew 8:5–13). When Jesus agreed, the centurion revealed his faith by saying, "Just say the word, and my servant will be healed." This man then went on to reveal his understanding of how authority works. He said, "For I, too, am a man under authority, with soldiers under me; and I say to this one, 'Go!' and he goes, and to another, 'Come!' and he comes, and to my slave, 'Do this!' and he does it." This military commander understood that his authority came from the fact that he, himself, was *under* authority. Jesus commended this man and did as he requested.

God's purpose in commanding us to obey the Word is not to confine us within some tight package, but to unleash spiritual power in our lives. One's access to change and ability to overcome are determined by one's response to God's Word. We will never experience the reality of God's statements until we act upon them. In fact, we will never really know who we *are* until we obey what we know. It is through obedience that spiritual realities and biblical promises are brought to life in us. We become a living fulfillment of what God has said.

Where we are in our relationship with God is once again the key factor. A certain level of trust must exist before we will be genuinely willing to yield control of life to someone else. Trust is progressive. The transfer of control in one's life is not automatic, nor is it instantaneous. Our relationship with God will be tested repeatedly in this arena.

Intimate Communication

Spiritual power is unleashed through prayer. The disciples recognized that the power in Jesus' life was somehow tied to prayer. The only time the Scriptures record them asking for a training seminar, the topic was "prayer."

I am convinced that the most powerful activity with which we will ever become involved is prayer. I am not referring to the trifling grocery list of mundane concerns we often bring before God, asking for a life that is successful, convenient, and problem-free. Rather, it is proactive, strategic prayer that draws the spiritual sword from its sheath. This kind of prayer sends shockwaves through the spirit world. Author Samuel Chadwick recognized this and wrote, "The one concern of the devil is to keep saints from praying. He fears nothing from prayerless studies, prayerless work, prayerless religion. He laughs at our toil, mocks at our wisdom, but he trembles when we pray."[2]

During my tour of duty in Vietnam, I flew as a copilot/technical observer in Mohawks (surveillance aircraft). They were fairly fast, highly maneuverable, and fun to fly. It surprised me to discover that this particular aircraft was one of the weapons the Vietnamese feared most. It was obviously not because of its awesome appearance. These were rather odd-looking airplanes with a bulbous nose and stubby wings. It was not because they were loaded with a deadly arsenal of guns and bombs. They carried only a few rockets for self-defense, and I am not certain we would have known how to use them if an opportunity ever presented itself.

What was so fearsome about these little olive-drab spy planes was their ability to recognize a problem and communicate with an unseen power that could eliminate the problem. The Vietnamese knew that when they heard the distinctive sound of our turboprops, even if they didn't see us fly overhead, it was only a matter of minutes before Phantom jets, Cobra helicopters, or various forms of artillery would rain down destruction upon them.

Correspondingly, there is nothing impressive about our human appearance either (sorry) and nothing inherently powerful within us. But the ability to communicate with the most awesome power in the universe makes us a formidable force within God's kingdom plan. The spirit world knows that when it hears the distinctive sound of God's people in prayer, the Almighty's hand is about to move, every single time.

God is preparing us to reign with him in his kingdom. Prayer is one of God's primary means of training us in the use of spiritual power. We are learning to wield power while under authority. The instructions for prayer indicate that unless we are under the authority of God and his Word, prayer is nothing more than mumbling to ourselves with our heads bowed. The instructions include placing ourselves in a position of dependence upon God, allowing the Word to dominate our thinking (John 15:7), using Jesus' name as our authority for bringing any requests (John 14:13), making our requests dependent upon God's will (Matthew 6:7–13) and focused on God's interests (Matthew 6:33). As we learn to reign, we reclaim the nobility that was lost in the Fall. Through intimacy, we experience the power that we have inherited as a child of the King. God has great plans for his children, plans that include crowns of authority, royal robes, and the thrill of reigning that we can only begin to imagine.

What Does Spiritual Power Look Like?

Jesus' ministry was characterized by power. Up to the age of thirty, there is no indication that he ever did any "power stunts." I don't believe Jesus' classmates ever ran home saying, "Wow, Mom! You should've seen what that Jesus kid did today!" But once his three-year ministry was launched, things began to happen. Water was turned to wine, food was multiplied, and storms were hushed. Better yet, the sick were healed. The blind received their sight. The dead were raised, and the spirit world was enraged as demons were dislodged and dethroned.

The power operating within Jesus not only had an effect on the world around him; it was the controlling factor of Jesus' personal life. It was a power that warded off temptation. He didn't cave in to destructive shortcuts and self-satisfying passions. He experienced a power that kept legitimate anger from expressing itself in sinful behavior. We never find Jesus coming apart at the seams or acting out of control. The power operating within him kept the pressure of his mission from overwhelming him. He knew what lay before him and yet had the strength to remain on task to the end. Although the Messiah was presented with a humble appearance and a gentle manner, there was no doubt that this man was the Lion of Judah, a man of power and authority like none before or since.

Some demote spiritual power to the level of the bizarre. In some circles, it has been reduced to unintelligible babble, hysterical laughing, and questionable healings. But spiritual power is not best seen in the dramatic or exotic. Such manifestations are worthless and meaningless in the practical scheme of things. The cry of the heart is not for flashes of spiritual ecstasy, but for the ability to experience life as God intended it to be lived.

Changing Life's Patterns

The most dramatic evidence of spiritual power is in a life that has changed and is changing. Even in an individual who has been known as a good person with a pleasant personality, there is a very real and observable transformation that accompanies salvation. If there is no change in one who claims new life in Christ, there is reason to question the authenticity of that claim. Initial changes occur at the time we give our life to the Savior. These changes confirm the fact that we are indeed saved. The specific changes God chooses to bring are as unique as the person in whom they occur. Just what it is that changes is not as significant as the fact that the transformation process has begun. There is identifiable evidence of power. It may show up in how one treats a spouse, family members, or work associates. It may surface as a change in vocabulary or in how one chooses to fill the hours in a day. Power is unmistakably present in the conquering of addictions and passions and in the transforming of destructive habits. It is the practical outworking of the process described in Ephesians 4:22–24:

> In reference to your former manner of life, you lay aside the old self, which is being corrupted in accordance with the lusts of deceit, and that you be renewed in the spirit of your mind, and put on the new self, which in the likeness of God has been created in righteousness and holiness of the truth.

Then there are ongoing changes that continue for the rest of our lives. God will never run out of issues to address within us. The personal glitches that constantly confound our efforts to live successfully are pinned down, one at a time, and overhauled. God's Spirit moves through each of our priorities and motivations, some of which we have consciously justified and others to which we have been oblivious. As we draw close to God, the Spirit probes our attitudes and each of the thoughts that contribute to our reactions to life. God lays hold of our habits (our default modes of thinking, feeling, and acting) and says, "These must change." Yahweh understands the defeated emotions of those caught in the grip of addictions and compulsions, whether they take the form of chemicals or food, perfectionism or pornography, work schedules or play schedules. To each of these God says, "This too must change. I will make it possible." The fact that change is taking place — genuine, lasting change — is a display of power that is envied by a powerless world.

Overcoming Life's Obstacles

Power is also revealed in how we respond to life itself. The problems and pressures common to everyone provide the setting for one of the most impressive displays of power. The Bible describes us in terms of fragile clay pottery. If empty, we are vulnerable — easily broken. But when our hollowness is filled with his holiness, we can endure the intensity of life and not be crushed by it:

> We have this treasure [Jesus Christ] in earthen vessels, that the surpassing greatness of the power may be of God and not from ourselves. (2 Corinthians 4:7)

The USS *Thresher* (SSN-593) was commissioned for service on August 3, 1961. The vessel "was the newest of the new, the first of a class designed to find and destroy other submarines in the deep ocean. She was the most advanced nuclear submarine American science and technology could produce — the pride of the Navy and of the men who served her."[3] On April 10, 1963, *Thresher* was performing a test dive 260 miles off the coast of New England. The plan was to spend six hours submerged and reach a test depth of one thousand feet. *Thresher* had never tried to deballast at test depth but had relied solely on her tremendous power to return to the surface. At 8:35 A.M., the escort ship, *Skylark*, received a message, "Proceeding to test depth." *Thresher* "was then sliding over the edge of the Continental Shelf, past a very steep cliff with a sheer drop of well over a mile. From now on, no rescue gear known to man could help her if she got into trouble. She must rely entirely on her own resources to regain the surface."[4]

Shortly after 9:00 A.M. the captain reported to the escort ship, "Experiencing minor difficulty. Have positive up-angle. Attempting to blow." Moments later, after *Thresher* sank to a depth of perhaps two thousand feet, *Skylark* received a garbled message, "We are exceeding test depth." At that moment, the boat imploded with the force of a ton of dynamite. *Thresher,* along with its crew of 129 brave men, was lost.

In order to find *Thresher*'s remains, the Navy deployed a bathyscaph, a small submersible designed to withstand the immense pressure of the water as it probed the ocean floor, miles below the surface. As they descended to *Thresher's* resting place, they found thousands of mangled pieces of wreckage. The sub had gone too deep. The pressure had become too great. The vessel had imploded.

Yet, while viewing the devastation, the crew of the bathyscaph occasionally noticed a passing fish. What was so amazing was that these sea creatures had no mighty hulls to protect them from being crushed. How could they survive with such fragile bodies and a paper-thin skin? The key to their survival is that the pressure on the inside of their body is the same as that on the outside.

To keep from being crushed by the pressures of deep-water living, we need more than just our own personal strength and a positive attitude. We must fill the inner person with something that can provide an equal and opposite pressure. This doesn't mean that we won't experience pressure. But it does mean that we won't be crushed by it.

As we learn from 2 Corinthians 4:7–9, the resident power of Jesus' life in us binds our emotions to a stronger heart when confusion reigns in our thoughts. It shields our fragile ego and prevents us from being shattered when we crash against the rugged unfairness of life. It provides uncompromising certainties in an unpredictable world, making it possible for us to rise from the ashes of the worst this world can offer.

Conclusion

I am convinced that God does not intend for his people to live painless, undisturbed lives. Rather, God longs for us to live a powerful life marked by sustained change and an unfolding freedom from the dysfunctions of an old life. God provides the capacity to cope with the tough things life throws at us and actually forces us to experience truth through those circumstances. God has not intended for his power to lie in some dormant form, untapped, unknown in the personal experience of his people.

Anaerobic living reveals that we are not properly connected to the source of inner strength. God has designed us to handle life with divine resources, not our own. The pulse of our heart is a reality check. We are to know firsthand "the surpassing greatness of His power toward us who believe" (Ephesians 1:19). We are to be "strengthened with all power, according to His glorious might" (Colossians 1:11).

Drawing Closer

1. In what ways have you experienced each of the challenges mentioned in 2 Corinthians 4:8–9? How has intimacy with God been a factor in your experience?

2. How would you differentiate between your own power and the power God expresses in your life?

3. Describe one way God has displayed his power in your life in the past six months. Do you see God's power more in overcoming obstacles or in personal change?

4. What do you believe is the greatest hindrance to spiritual power in your life? How do you plan to address this hindrance?

5. What is your opinion of the quotation from Samuel Chadwick on page 156? If it is true, why is it true?

TWELVE

Good Things Run Wild

(living extreme integrity among wandering values)

W HILE ON THE STAFF OF A LARGE CHURCH, A FRIEND OF MINE developed a close friendship with the senior pastor of that ministry. One day, as they sat in the senior's office talking about the trivia of life, this pastor leaned back in his chair and pointed to an untitled leather-bound book assigned to an inconspicuous location among other books of similar size and color. "That's my personal journal," he explained. "Obviously, it contains some very private thoughts. My inner struggles and personal failures, many of which are unknown to anyone else on the face of this earth, are detailed in that book. Good friend, if anything ever happens to me, I want you to destroy that book. No one needs to know what is written on those pages."

We have all done things that we know are wrong. We have acted in ways that are immoral or unethical. We have intentionally hurt people and consciously disobeyed rules. We may have even dabbled in at least one of what I consider to be the top ten sins of our time: alcoholism, pornography, child abuse, chronic lying, sex outside of marriage, gluttony, homosexuality, abortion, drug abuse, and materialism. If we haven't, we have certainly thought about it.

As he opens his second letter, the apostle Peter lays out a master plan for the Christian life. He begins by describing the amazing commitment God has made to us. Everything that could possibly be needed to live successfully as a child of God has been lavishly provided. Every contingency has been considered and accounted for. All that remains is to do it. There is no acceptable excuse. According to Peter, it is completely our choice.

The apostle then outlines a sequence for developing spiritual character. He is careful to use terminology making it clear that these steps are not automatic. They require decisions, and they will cost something. These items are not an inventory of preinstalled luxuries to be enjoyed, but a roster of expectations anticipated in every believer. With that, the list begins. At the top of that list, number one, first thing out of the chute: "moral excellence" (2 Peter 1:5).

Moral excellence goes by many names. In the Bible it is a component of godliness and righteousness. It is being above reproach and without blame. Apart from the Scriptures, it is virtue and character. In derogatory terms, it is referred to as being prudish, Victorian, or legalistic. At the bottom line, moral excellence is an uncompromising commitment to what is good and right.

I use the phrase "encoded ethics" to describe the moral standard that has been imprinted on our hearts. It is the opposite of random, impulsive living. In contrast to a world driven by feelings, encoded ethics describes a life that is anchored to something solid. What is right and wrong has been settled in the heart. Personal boundaries have been established, and a course of action has been predetermined. Movement through a day is not capricious but marked by a loving connectedness to the Ruler of the universe. A powerful purity lived out in courageous character, moral excellence is unmistakably visible and undeniably attractive.

By way of contrast, it should never surprise us when unsaved people act unsaved with self-destructive behavior, failed marriages, emotions out of control, lying and cheating, caught up in materialism, humanism, and hedonism. Such a life is normal, although sad, for someone apart from Christ. But it should deeply trouble us when saved people (including ourselves) continue their old patterns of life. We have been given an entirely new life that is to be displayed in a moral transformation.

Bedrock in the practical expression of new life in Christ is a clean break with the old one. It's not just a matter of sprucing up one's lifestyle or of making a few adjustments to one's value system. In coming to Christ, the old life was junked. It's over! The person one was is deceased, not "in the process" of dying. It's just a fact (Romans

6:1–7). Think about the implications. For example, dead people do not have to be rehabilitated; they just have to be buried.

This new behavior is not driven by a set of rules. It is not a legalistic checklist that results in some kind of self-righteous achievement badge. Rather than an effort to win God's approval, the new behavior is evidence that we have already received it. It is simply living as one who is loved so completely that there is no need to seek degrading substitutes; it is practical freedom from self-destructive lusts and visible proof that we are no longer believing the misinformation and disinformation that pervades the thinking of a fallen world. The inner code has been changed.

The Moral Code

We live in a time when many do not believe there are any legitimate moral standards. Tim Keller writes, "We do not live in an immoral society — one in which right and wrong are clearly understood and wrong behavior is chosen. We live in an amoral society — one in which 'right' and 'wrong' are categories with no universal meaning, and everyone 'does what is right in his or her own eyes.' "[1] Yet the Bible says it is impossible fully to escape God's moral code:

> That which is known about God is evident within them; for God made it evident to them…they know the ordinance of God. (Romans 1:19,32)

I once took a polygraph (lie detector) test. I wanted to know how the contraption worked, so I visited the local police and asked them to do a harmless interrogation of an "innocent" pastor. This was an unprecedented request. They weren't convinced that there might not be a regulation somewhere that prohibited such a demonstration, but they agreed to give it a try. I was seated in a room straight out of a movie set, with blank walls, a table, a few uncomfortable chairs, and a single light hanging from the ceiling. An officer brought in the machinery and taped sensors to various places on my head and arms. Each of these had wires running back to the machine. The event began to attract a crowd, and soon the room was filled with officers and staff, while others watched through a window. I was first asked some basic questions to calibrate the device: name, address, what I ate for breakfast. He then showed me the red line meandering along a six-inch-wide highway of paper that slowly fed itself out onto the table. "This is what truth and honesty look like," he explained.

Then he asked me the same set of questions but wanted me to intentionally lie about each one and to do so with a "straight" face. As I did, I could see the needle move toward the edge of the paper strip. Even though I felt no sense of guilt over these comments, my body was still reacting to that which I knew was wrong. As the atmosphere in the room lightened, some officers suggested that they ask me about my personal life and my driving habits. At that point, I decided that I had seen enough!

Everyone has a degree of knowledge about what is right and wrong (Romans 1:18–25). What makes the encoded ethics of a believer's life so attractive is not the awareness of a standard, but the application of it. Actually living by God's principles allows for a clear conscience. The guilt-producing aspects of life are drastically reduced. An incredible freedom comes with such living. We don't have to live in fear that someone will find our personal journal and disclose its contents. Sir Arthur Conan Doyle, author of the Sherlock Holmes stories, once played a prank on nine of his friends. He sent them each a telegram that simply read, "Flee at once! All is known!" Within a few hours, they had all left the country.

One of the most exhilarating sensations I have experienced comes with the awareness that I have consciously done what is right. There is the satisfaction of pleasing my heavenly Father and the confirmation that I really am a new creation in Christ. The feeling of new life reverberates throughout my entire being. Prompting this feeling is not so much the action itself, but its rightness. It matches who I am and fulfills the deepest longings of my heart. It feels clean. It's exciting! G. K. Chesterton observed, "The more I considered Christianity, I discovered that while it established a rule and order, the chief end of that order was to give room for good things to run wild in me."

Encoded ethics brings a structure to the life of a believer. It defines the boundaries, includes details of how to make life work properly and enjoyably, and sets forth the consequences for violating the rules of life. As a result, we are set free to experience life as God intended it. Albert Einstein wrote, "The most important human endeavor is the striving for morality in our actions. Our inner balance, and even our very existence depends on it. Only morality in our actions can give beauty and dignity to our lives."[2] By living according to God's standard, we are not encumbered with the fallout of mismanaged life. The Scriptures exhort us,

> Let us also lay aside every encumbrance, and the sin which so easily entangles us, and let us run with endurance the race that is set before us. (Hebrews 12:1)

How Does Intimacy Produce Integrity?

By Creating a Difference from One's Old Life

It would be wonderful if all we needed for transformation was a sprinkling of angel dust and — poof! Reality is much different. The encoding process begins in the mind, by changing our thinking. The Bible spells it out in these words: "Do not be conformed to this world, but be transformed by the renewing of your mind" (Romans 12:2). It is programming the conscience, that internal monitor of the heart.

Our conscience should give us an accurate Bible-centered analysis of what is going on inside us. The conscience was designed to make us feel the same way about sin as God does. Proper programming, or encoding, of the conscience includes a proper understanding of both the gravity of sin and the grace of God.

The gravity of sin. Facing the gravity of sin is a violently painful and intensely personal experience. We are confronted with it in the pages of Scripture and in the ravages of life itself. The latter was the experience of Yehiel Dinur, "a small haggard man...who had miraculously escaped death in Auschwitz."

Adolf Eichmann was one of the worst of the Holocaust masterminds. When he stood trial, prosecutors called a string of former concentration camp prisoners as witnesses....On his day to testify, Dinur entered the courtroom and stared at the man behind the bulletproof glass — the man who had presided over the slaughter of millions. As the eyes of the two men met — victim and murderous tyrant — the courtroom fell silent, filled with the tension of the confrontation.

Then suddenly, Yehiel Dinur began to sob, collapsing to the floor. Was he overcome by hatred...by the horrifying memories...by the evil incarnate in Eichmann's face?

No. As he later explained in an interview, it was because Eichmann was not the demonic personification of evil Dinur had expected. Rather, he was an ordinary man, just like anyone else. And in that one instant, Dinur came to the stunning realization that sin and evil are the human condition. "I was afraid about myself," Dinur said. "I saw that I am capable to do this...exactly like he."[3]

Until we have seen sin for what it is — deadly, horrifying, and sickeningly repulsive — we will never feel the urgency to escape nor appreciate the grace that makes such an escape possible. The Bible teaches that the closer we get to God, the more we will become aware of our own sin. The prophet Isaiah experienced this in a dramatic fashion. Finding himself in the presence of the holy God, Isaiah became aware of his own sin and cried, "Woe is me, for I am ruined!" (Isaiah 6:5).

But in an odd twist of truth, the further we get from God, the more we will become aware of the sins of others. Attention is diverted from our own failures and inadequacies to those of others. We go about adjusting standards to fit personal weaknesses. C. S. Lewis observed that "when a man is getting better, he understands more and more clearly the evil that is still left in him. When a man is getting worse, he understands his own badness less and less. A moderately bad man knows he is not very good; a thoroughly bad man thinks he is alright [sic]."[4]

The grace of God. Recently, I attended an Antiquarian Booksellers Faire. I realize that may not sound like a thrilling way to spend a Saturday, but I enjoy old books, and the faire was promoted with some classy advertisements. What I found was fascinating — thousands of old leather-bound volumes, many of which had dramatic histories. Among them were the personal journals of historic personalities, some famous, some obscure. I am certain that none of them ever dreamed their private thoughts and confessions would be read by strangers and sold for thousands of dollars.

It is amazing what people were willing to pay for those old books. I once heard that the value of anything is determined by what someone is willing to pay for it. In the case of those old books, the transactions were setting their value. Their established worth was staggering.

When Jesus died on the cross, he established the value of those for whom he died. At an infinite cost to himself, he purchased all those beat-up "living" books — lives that filled pages of journals with the cruel realities of sin. On each page, he has written the word "forgiven" across our failures. Between the lines, Jesus has written his own story of grace.

The word "conscience" means "to have knowledge with" or "to be in agreement with" or "to see together with" something. Depending upon how we have programmed our conscience, we will either be justified or condemned by our actions. Ultimately, if our actions agree with God, his character, and his standard, then we have a clear conscience and experience inner peace.

We encode the ethics of our life by meditating on God's Word. This practice underwrites the *what*'s and *how*'s of our life patterns with substantial *why*'s. By thinking through the probable situations we might encounter and linking them to biblical principles, we predetermine a course of action that we know is in agreement with God's standard. We must set personal limits (boundaries), deciding before we are confronted with a decision what things we will and will not do. The motivation to take such action is based upon our movement toward God.

By Creating a Distance from One's Old Life

Border riding is common but deadly. Often, we attempt to live our new life in Christ too close to our old life. Having made a decision to give our life to Christ, we can choose to set up camp just across the line. From that vantage point, it is easy to gaze back into our former life and imagine that it wasn't all that bad. Because it is so accessible, we can find ourselves making forays back into old failures. We need to move away from the danger zone and increase the distance between ourselves and our old lifestyles. It is foolish to always live on the verge of failure.

There is a way of living that has become natural to each of us: default routines that require no thought, well-worn paths with which we have become comfortable. This certain way of approaching life and responding to circumstances is just "us." Then there is the way of living to which God has called us. It is unnatural and uncomfortable. Because it is not routine, it requires conscious, repeated effort.

So how can we create distance from that old life? While there are many things over which we have little or no control, we can indeed determine certain very significant factors in our personal environment. The people we surround ourselves with, the social settings, the work arrangements, and our private time are all filled with choices. We decide with whom we will spend leisure time and whom we will count as a friend. These are people we allow to affect our thinking and our behavior. While it is true that we are called to make significant contact with the unsaved world around us, these are not to be the people who shape our thinking. If our moral code is being jammed by those we call our friends, then we need to change friends.

Social environment. It is foolish to consciously place ourselves in settings that play into our known weaknesses. It is foolish to remain in a social setting when we see a morally dangerous scenario unfolding. The Bible tells us to "flee from youthful lusts" (2 Timothy 2:22). In plain language that means to get out of any situations where temptation poses a risk to one's moral health. That risk, by the way, is almost always greater than we assess it to be.

Work environment. If we are faced with questionable business practices, with issues of greed (personal or corporate), or with morally corrupt fellow employees or business partners, we may need to change our workplace. We may even need to consider changing our occupation. Such actions obviously have personal and financial implications. Family stability may be jolted and a career may be jeopardized. But in the process, the reality of our claims to spiritual intimacy is displayed in high relief.

Private time. Our greatest hazard may be when we are alone and no one can see what we do. We may need to build personal fences to insure that we do not buckle under the weight of such freedom. It is too easy to cave in to a personal vice when there is nobody to see our actions. We may need to plan our private time and take decisive action to guard against our own wicked heart.

What Does Integrity Look Like?

Keep your behavior excellent among the Gentiles, so that in the thing in which they slander you as evildoers, they may on account of your good deeds, as they observe them, glorify God in the day of visitation.... For such is the will of God that by doing right you may silence the ignorance of foolish men. (1 Peter 2:12,15)

Peter reminds these believers that they are being watched. An unsaved world is convinced that new life in Christ is a sham and is expecting them to crash like everyone else. Foolish people who have held God at a distance are waiting, and at times hoping, for God's people to fail. Peter tells believers that their actions will silence such people and draw attention to the great work God has done in them.

Intimacy with God is recognized by a clean break from an old life. It involves a complete moral and ethical overhaul. One's old life, along with its destructive modes of operation, is replaced by a new life. The apostle Paul described it with these words:

If any man is in Christ, he is a new creature; the old things passed away; behold, new things have come. (2 Corinthians 5:17)

Before coming to Christ, these destructive behaviors made sense. They were desperate attempts to fill the emptiness inside, hide the guilt of personal failures, and take away the dull throb of loneliness. They were expressions of our anger at life and our alienation from God. But now they no longer fit with who we are. God has removed the guilt and filled the emptiness. Yahweh has drawn us close and loved us jealously. God has written his Word into our hearts, encoding it with his own breath. Now it only makes sense to disengage from a worthless facade and recast our character in light of what God has done. Our life in Christ should clearly reveal the death of an old life and the birth of a new one. It must be a clean break that touches every aspect of our life.

Sexual Compromise

At the head of the list, I would put a clean break from *sexual compromise*. This means that we are not involved in any sexual activity outside of marriage — not before, not during, not after (in the case of a death or divorce) — not ever.

This moral position encompasses more than the concluding act of sex itself; that is, it includes all the peripheral activities as well. It means that we don't communicate, knowingly or naively, that we might be open to sexual compromise. Our manner of dress, facial expressions, and type of conversations can all send signals that we might be a willing participant in some kind of sexual liaison. It means that we don't give ourselves the freedom to entertain romantic fantasies that would not be honoring to our Savior. It means that we don't feed our minds with pornography, whether it be the hard-core material found in "adult" bookstores, dingy theaters, and X-rated Web sites or the more subtle forms found in respectable bookstores, upscale theaters, and television soaps and sitcoms.

Substance Abuse

New life in Christ also calls for a clean break from *substance abuse*. This means that we don't allow ourselves to be a slave to food, drugs, or alcohol. It means that we take our freedom in Christ seriously and guard it jealously. It means that we don't knowingly put ourselves in compromising situations that could lead to wrong actions, especially when we are aware of specific weaknesses within us. It means that we do more than just scale back. If our life is being controlled by one or more of these substances, we must deal decisively and completely with the problem. We must stop perpetuating it through self-denial and self-deception.

Michel Quoist writes, "If your body makes all the decisions and gives all the orders, and if you obey, the physical can effectively destroy every other dimension of your personality. Your emotional life will be blunted and your spiritual life will be stifled and ultimately will become anemic."[5] In 1 Corinthians 9:27, Paul writes,

> I buffet my body and make it my slave, lest possibly, after I have preached to others, I myself should be disqualified.

Business Fraud

New life in Christ shows up in a clean break from *business fraud*. This means bringing honesty into our business dealings. With this separation, we are not involved in cheating, swindling, or taking advantage of the unsuspecting. Paul instructs believers to "respect what is right in the sight of all men" (Romans 12:17). It means choosing to do what is right even when it may mean losing a business deal, a promotion, or possibly a job. It means choosing to operate on the basis of something other than greed. It means doing our best work for a fair price. It means logging honest hours and keeping accurate books.

Bringing honesty to our business dealings means not just being less dishonest, but being *completely* honest. Bob Briner addresses business-people with these words, "Integrity is not something you are born with, but something you must earn. And keep. All it takes is one wrong move for your reputation to be damaged. Most of us really do know the difference between right and wrong, but it's all too easy to see the good that might come from an unethical choice."[6]

Vocal Trash

The moral excellence of new life means a clean break from *vocal trash*, which means we are increasingly free from swearing as well as from crude and immoral jokes. We are not laughing and encouraging such conversation in others. We are increasingly setting the moral tone of conversations. It means that we are fulfilling the instructions of Ephesians 4:29,

> Let no unwholesome word proceed from your mouth, but only such a word as is good for edification according to the need of the moment, that it may give grace to those who hear.

The term "unwholesome" is one that was used during biblical times to describe rotten fish. In other words, our communication shouldn't stink. Our language should be free from put-downs, innuendos, racial slurs, and the general four-letter variety of terms. Instead, our words should be refreshing and encouraging to those around us.

Physical Violence

A clean break from *physical violence* is also a part of the display of new life. Doing what is right includes defending the helpless and actively assuring the fair treatment of others. It means that we are never striking someone out of anger or frustration. It means that we are not physically out of control, harming those around us. It means that others feel safe in our presence . . . especially our spouse and our children. Acts of kindness and mercy are what they experience.

The Living Code

As you read through the Gospels, you always find Jesus doing the most appropriate thing in any situation. While he was notoriously unpredictable, his actions were in perfect harmony with his purpose — glorifying the Father. Jesus read life in light of biblical realities and could see God's fingerprints on every situation.

Jesus never waffled on issues of right and wrong, good and evil. He exposed corruption and commended character. He questioned personal values and applauded personal sacrifice. Jesus labeled the hypocritical Pharisees as whitewashed tombs and the greedy temple merchants as thieves. He challenged those who withheld good deeds on spiritual technicalities and exposed others whose "good" actions were driven by selfish motives.

Jesus modeled the awesome liberty of a guilt-free life. He never had sleepless nights regretting shameful actions. He had nothing to hide, so he could be perfectly open with others. He was a man of such integrity that people took him at his word and never questioned whether he would be faithful to what he said.

In Jesus' presence, the moral and ethical lives of people were flipped upside down. Corrupt tax gatherers returned their graft with interest, and sleazy prostitutes repented in tears. Jesus offered them a chance to start all over again, often sending them away with the words, "Go, and sin no more."

Conclusion

It may help to picture ourselves as the spiritual beggars that we are. Ruth A. Walton penned the following parable in an effort to portray what we miss by hanging on to the "rags" that are characteristic of a life lived distant from God.

> Once a beggar lived near the King's palace. One day as he passed the palace he saw a proclamation posted outside the palace gate. The King

was giving a great dinner. Anyone who was dressed in royal garments was invited to the party.

The beggar went on his way but he kept thinking about the royal banquet and how he would like to attend. He looked at the rags he was wearing and sighed. Surely only kings and their families wore royal robes, he thought.

Slowly an idea crept into his mind. The audacity of it made him tremble. Would he dare? An overwhelming desire to attend the feast took hold of him and he made his way back to the palace. His whole body shook as he approached the guard at the gate. "Please, Sire, I would like to speak to the King."

"And what is your business?" asked the guard.

"I would like to speak to him about the banquet," said the beggar. The guard opened the gate and let the beggar through. Quickly he led him inside the palace.

"Wait here," he said. In a few minutes he was back. "His Majesty will see you," he said and led the beggar into a large room where the King sat.

The beggar approached the King, bent low and murmured, "Greetings, Your Majesty."

"You wished to see me?" asked the King.

"Yes, Your Majesty. You see, I want so much to attend the banquet but as you know I have no royal robes to wear. Please, Sir, if I be so bold, may I have one of your old garments so that I, too, may come to the banquet?" The beggar trembled and shook so hard that he could not see the faint smile that was on the King's face.

"You have been wise in coming to the only one who could supply you with the necessary garments," the King said. He called to his Son, the young prince. "Take this man to your room and array him in some of your clothes." The Prince did as he was told and soon the beggar was standing before a mirror, clothed in garments that he had never dared dream he would someday wear.

"You are now eligible to attend the King's banquet tomorrow night," said the Prince. "But even more important, you will never need another set of clothes. These garments will last forever. You will always belong to royalty."

The beggar dropped to his knees. "Oh, thank you, thank you," he cried. But as he started to leave the room he looked back at his pile of dirty rags lying on the floor. He hesitated. What if what the Prince said was not true? What if he would need his old clothes again? Quickly he gathered up his old garments. Clinging to them, he followed the Prince.

The banquet was far greater than he had ever imagined but he could not enjoy himself as he should. He had made a small bundle of his old rags and it kept falling off his lap as he sat at the table. The food was passed quickly and the beggar missed some the greatest delicacies as he struggled to hang on to his bundle of rags.

Time proved that the Prince was right. The clothes lasted forever, staying just as beautiful as they were the first time the beggar wore them. Still the poor beggar grew fonder and fonder of his old rags and could not part with them.

As time passed people seemed to forget the royal robes he was wearing. They saw only the little bundle of filthy rags that he clung to wherever he went. Whenever they talked of him they always spoke of the old man with the bundle of rags. The royal robes seemed unimportant.

One day as he lay dying, the King visited him. The beggar saw the sad look on the King's face when he saw the small bundle of rags by the bed. Suddenly the beggar remembered the Prince's words and he realized that his bundle of rags had cost him a lifetime of true royalty. He wept bitterly at his folly.

And the King wept with him.[7]

It is a common tendency to drag the rags of our old life through our remaining years on earth. I admit that I am not exempt from this (I wish I were). But don't go looking for *my* journal. I have made a point of *not* keeping one. I'm sure it exists in the libraries of heaven, but in God's eyes my private journal has undergone some editing. It now tells a story of incredible grace.

Drawing Closer

1. Describe how distance from God affects how you feel about your own personal sin. How does moving closer to God change that?

2. In which areas of your life do you find yourself living too close to your old routines? How does that affect your relationship with God?

3. How have you experienced God's graceful forgiveness in your life? What led to that experience? How has that experience changed you?

4. In what areas of your life do you justify what is wrong by presuming that God will forgive you? How do you think this affects your conscience?

5. What might you be missing today because of a tendency to hang on to some old rags?

Three Vital Questions

(flirting with the future)

NOW THAT WE HAVE TRAVELED TOGETHER FOR AWHILE, WHAT HAS been accomplished? Has the discussion fueled your passion for God? Has the pathway been marked clearly enough? Does an ever closer relationship with God seem more realistic than it did twelve chapters ago? Better yet, are you beginning to experience intimacy with God as presented in those chapters?

I offered a disclaimer in the introduction to this book. I stated that I wrote this book, not because I have all the answers, but as a part of my own search for them. I can assure you that while you have been processing the thoughts on these pages, I have continued to do the same. As a parting gift, let me offer you three questions I have found to be of great value in my own quest for intimacy with God. They are questions I try to ask myself each day.

- What am I doing?

- Why am I doing it?

- Is it worthy of praise?

While answering these questions will never ensure the integrity of my spiritual journey with Christ, the failure to subject myself to their scrutiny virtually guarantees my ruin. It is certainly possible, and far too often the practice, to devise answers that will justify my own selfish actions. I know this very well. But I also know that when asked by an honest heart, when asked in the face of God's Word, when asked in the presence of the God I long to know, these questions can blow away the self-imposed smoke that obscures my view of God.

What Am I Doing?

What do my actions reveal about me? More importantly, what do they reveal about the life-transforming Savior I claim to know? What am I doing at this moment or any other point in a given day? Is it right? Could it be seen as a living fulfillment of the Scriptures? Is what I am doing, in both the broad strokes and the blunt details, a pattern worthy for others to follow? Do my actions make it easy for my Lord to bless me? Are they genuinely pleasing to God? Do they draw me closer to God or create relational distance between us?

Why Am I Doing It?

It is a sobering thought that I can be doing the right things for the wrong reasons. It is not enough simply to do what is right. It can, in fact, be deadly. I have found that pride and self-righteousness infiltrate virtually every "right" action in my life. They settle in rather quietly at first, inflating my ego. They continue in their pleasantly self-affirming manner until challenged by an unappreciative comment or a disturbing question, a question like "Why?" Can I honestly say that my actions are motivated by a desire to enrich my relationship with God and to put that connectedness into visible terms? Or am I acting for my own glory, for my own personal fulfillment, for the praise of others, or even for their pity? The *why*'s of my actions are far more difficult to face than the *what*'s. I find it much harder to ask *why* than to ask *what*.

Is It Worthy of Praise?

I have been called to a life of excellence, and yet I willingly feed the patterns of mediocrity and dysfunction. I have been called to a race, a marathon, and yet I often find myself content to simply face the right direction and slowly shuffle my feet toward the finish line. Is this really the best I can offer? How can I be more effective for the King and his kingdom? I am not looking to become busier or to move life at a faster pace. I am not attempting to inflict guilt upon myself. But I do long, so very much, to hear the God I love say, "Well done, my good and faithful servant." You know, I don't believe God will speak those words to everyone. They will not be offered as a standard greeting to each person who steps into heaven.

A day is coming when I will stand before the one who has redeemed me, forgiven me, and set me free, the one who loves me passionately and has called me to live near him. On that day, there will be no doubt that I have a new identity and that the power and wealth of heaven are at my command. But on *that* day, what will I wish I had done on *this* day? As my Savior reviews the days of my life, I will not be surprised if he chooses to ask me these three questions:

- What did you do?
- Why did you do it?
- Was it really worthy of praise?

The answers to those questions will be determined by the answer to a question God has already asked:

> "Who is he who will devote himself
> to be close to me?" declares the LORD.
> —Jeremiah 30:21, NIV

Grace to you!

Notes

Chapter 1: Terms of Endearment

1. Paul Thigpen, "Closer than a Brother," *Discipleship Journal* 54 (1989): 30.
2. Ibid.
3. Borrowed from Ray S. Anderson, *Everything That Makes Me Happy* (Downers Grove, Ill.: InterVarsity Press, 1995), 147.
4. Lawrence J. Crabb Jr., *The Marriage Builder* (Grand Rapids, Mich.: Zondervan, 1982), 20.
5. Michael J. Wilkins, *In His Image* (Colorado Springs: NavPress, 1997), 89.
6. J. Oswald Sanders, *Enjoying Intimacy with God* (Chicago: Moody Press, 1980), 13–14.
7. Blaise Pascal, quoted by John Piper, *Desiring God* (Portland, Ore.: Multnomah Press, 1986), 16.
8. Blaise Pascal, quoted in *Leadership* (Fall 1994): 60.
9. This true story was originally told by Dr. James Fleming, a professor of archaeology in Jerusalem. I heard it from Dr. Ron Allen, a professor of Hebrew Scripture at Western Conservative Baptist Seminary.
10. J. I. Packer, quoted by Mark Tabb, "Where Do I Start?" *Moody Monthly* (January 1998): 17.
11. Brennan Manning, *Lion and Lamb* (Dallas: Word, 1986), 24.
12. C. S. Lewis, *The Silver Chair* (New York: HarperCollins, 1994), 20–21.
13. Ravi Zacharias, *Cries of the Heart* (Nashville: Word, 1998), 48.

Chapter 2: Points of Reference

1. Remi A. Nadeau, *Los Angeles: From Mission to Modern City* (New York: Longman, Green & Co., 1960), 71.
2. Ibid., 82.
3. Glenn S. Dumke, *The Boom of the Eighties in Southern California* (San Marino, Calif.: Huntington Library, 1944), 201.
4. Richard C. Halverson, *Christian Maturity* (Los Angeles: Cowman Publications, 1956), 9.

5. David C. Needham, *Birthright* (Portland, Ore.: Multnomah Press, 1979), 47.

6. Fred Smith, *You and Your Network* (Waco, Tex.: Word, 1984), 68.

7. Dick Keyes, *True Heroism* (Colorado Springs: NavPress, 1995), 13.

8. Michael J. Anthony, *The Effective Church Board* (Grand Rapids, Mich.: Baker, 1993), 138–39.

9. Buell H. Kazee, *Faith Is the Victory* (Wheaton, Ill.: Tyndale, 1983), 29, 37.

10. Irenaeus, quoted by Douglas Hall, *Imaging God* (Grand Rapids, Mich.: Eerdmans, 1986), 200.

Chapter 3: Facts of Life

1. My apology to the many wonderful senior flight attendants who are not like the one described in this chapter.

2. Composite thoughts from Ecclesiastes 3:11; Hebrews 4:16; 2 Peter 1: 2–11.

3. Composite thoughts from Psalm 34:1–22; Hebrews 3:12–15; Philippians 3:7–11.

4. Composite thoughts from Psalm 46:10; Matthew 11:28–30; Luke 10: 38–42.

5. Composite thoughts from Psalm 19:7–11; Jeremiah 9:23–24; 1 John 1: 3–4.

6. Composite thoughts from Psalm 40:1–8; Psalm 52:16–17; Philippians 4: 4–5.

7. Larry Crabb, *Inside Out* (Colorado Springs: NavPress, 1988), 32.

8. Marshall Shelley, *Well-Intentioned Dragons* (Waco, Tex.: Word, 1985), 11.

9. Philip Yancey, *Disappointment with God* (Grand Rapids, Mich.: Zondervan, 1988), 24.

Chapter 4: Gazing into the Eyes of God

1. Malcolm Muggeridge as quoted by Michael Phillips, *A God to Call Father* (Wheaton, Ill.: Tyndale, 1994), 182.

2. *Factoid* refers to data that a person has decided is a fact, while it may be or may not be.

3. Malcolm Muggeridge, "Christian Be Watchful," *His* (May 1973), 23.

4. Lewis Carroll, *Through the Looking Glass* (New York: Bantam, 1981), 157.

5. J. P. Moreland, *Love Your God with All Your Mind* (Colorado Springs: NavPress, 1997), 25.

6. Harry Verploegh, *Oswald Chambers* (Nashville: Oliver-Nelson Books, 1987), 110.

7. Jerry Bridges, *The Joy of Fearing God* (Colorado Springs: WaterBrook Press, 1997), 202.

8. Pat Westfall, "The Princess and the Tower," *His* (February 1978): 34.

Chapter 5: Dancing in the Arms of God

1. John McArthur, "The Other Six Days of the Week," *Moody Monthly* (February 1987): 64.

2. Eugene H. Peterson, *A Long Obedience* (Downers Grove, Ill.: InterVarsity Press, 1980), 50.

3. J. Oswald Sanders, *Enjoying Intimacy with God* (Chicago: Moody Press, 1980), 26.

4. Peterson, *A Long Obedience*, 52.

5. Richard J. Foster, *The Celebration of Discipline* (San Francisco: Harper and Row, 1978), 148.

6. Printed in *Focal Point*, a publication of Denver Seminary (September 1989).

7. Michael Wiebe, "Quiet Time and the Sunday Service," *His* (June 1979): 13.

8. Elizabeth Barrett Browning, "Aurora Leigh, Seventh Book."

9. For example, Hebrews 10:25 says, "Let us not give up meeting together" (NIV).

10. Tim Sims and Dan Pegoda, *101 Things to Do during a Dull Sermon* (Grand Rapids, Mich.: Zondervan, 1984), random samplings.

11. Ronald Allen and Gordon Borror, *Worship* (Portland, Ore.: Multnomah Press, 1982), 31.

12. David Needham, "What Do You Do with a God Too Big?" *Moody Monthly* (January 1984): 20.

13. Teri Loren, *The Dancer's Companion* (New York: Dial Press, 1978), 69.

14. Margaret H'Doubler, quoted by Margery J. Turner, *Dance Handbook* (Englewood Cliffs, N.J.: Prentice-Hall, 1959), 6.

15. Richard M. Stephenson and Joseph Iaccarino, *The Complete Book of Ballroom Dancing* (Garden City, N.Y.: Doubleday, 1980), 3.

16. Loren, *The Dancer's Companion*, 203–4.

Chapter 6: Delighting in the Mind of God

1. OK, so I know there aren't fairies, but there were when I was *that* age.

2. A. W. Tozer, *The Pursuit of God* (Harrisburg, Pa.: Christian Publications, 1948), 100.

3. Frank Buchman, "How to Listen," quoted by Klaus Bockmuehl, *Listening to the God Who Speaks* (Colorado Springs: Helmers and Howard, 1990), 8.

4. Francis A. Schaeffer, *The New Superspirituality* (Downers Grove, Ill.: InterVarsity Press, 1972), 16.

5. Malcolm Muggeridge, *Jesus: The Man Who Lives* (New York: Harper and Row, 1975), 8.

6. Malcolm Muggeridge, *A Twentieth-Century Testimony* (Nashville: Thomas Nelson, 1978), 72.

Chapter 7: Venturing into the Heart of God

1. "Coming Home to a Strange New Land," *The Economist*, 1 June 1991, 36.

2. Ruth Westheimer and Steven Kaplan, "Surviving Salvation," *OneWorld Magazine*.

3. Haddon W. Robinson, foreword to *Lifestyle Evangelism*, by Joseph C. Aldrich (Portland, Ore.: Multnomah Press, 1981), 11.

4. Sheldon Vanauken, *A Severe Mercy* (New York: Harper and Row, 1977), 85.

5. Jim Petersen, *Evangelism as a Lifestyle* (Colorado Springs: NavPress, 1980), 79.

6. Jacques Ellul, *The Subversion of Christianity* (Grand Rapids, Mich.: Eerdmans, 1986), 55.

7. William B. Allen, "You Must Open the Letters," *Alliance Witness*, 14 January 1976, 5.

8. Rebecca Manley Pippert, *Hope Has Its Reasons* (San Francisco: Harper and Row, 1989), 3.

9. Pippert, *Hope Has Its Reasons*, 90.

10. Joseph C. Aldrich, *Lifestyle Evangelism* (Portland, Ore.: Multnomah Press, 1981), 15–16. Used by permission of Multnomah Publishers, Inc.

Chapter 8: Marked for Life

1. See Matthew 22:34–40; Mark 12:28–31; Luke 10:25–37.

2. Richard C. Trench, *Synonyms of the New Testament* (Grand Rapids, Mich.: AP&A), 38–42.

3. Tertullian, *Apology*.

4. Francis A. Schaeffer, *The Mark of the Christian* (Downers Grove, Ill.: InterVarsity Press, 1970), 21.

5. Lawrence J. Crabb, *Understanding People* (Grand Rapids, Mich.: Zondervan, 1987), 199.

6. Jerry B. Jenkins, *Twelve Things* (Chicago: Moody Press, 1991), 24.

7. Francis of Sales, quoted in *Acts of Love* (Gresham, Ore.: Vision House Publications, 1994), 28.

8. See chapter 5 for how Jesus expressed joy in his life.

9. Henry Cloud and John Townsend, *Boundaries* (Grand Rapids, Mich.: Zondervan, 1992), 47.

10. C. S. Lewis, *The Four Loves* (New York: Harcourt, 1960), 169.

11. This is my own version of a short story by Max Beerbolm entitled "The Happy Hypocrite" (New York: John Lane Co., 1922).

Chapter 9: Intimate I-sight

1. Brian Crane, *Pickles*, Washington Post Writers Group, 9 September 1996.

2. C. S. Lewis, *Mere Christianity* (New York: Macmillan, 1952), 106.

3. Joseph M. Stowell, *Perilous Pursuits* (Chicago: Moody Press, 1994), 149.

4. Joni Eareckson Tada, "At the Foot of the Cross," *Discipleship Journal* (May/June 1998): 50.

5. P. T. Forsyth, quoted by Ray Comfort, *Hell's Best Kept Secret* (Springdale, Ill.: Whitaker House, 1989), 17.

6. "Spiritishness" is a word I have coined (don't bother trying to look it up!) to suggest the contrast between a self-centered life and a Spirit-centered life.

7. Francis A. Schaeffer, *True Spirituality* (Wheaton, Ill.: Tyndale, 1971), 9.

8. Bill Hybels, *Descending into Greatness* (Grand Rapids, Mich.: Zondervan, 1993), 17.

9. Adaptation of story retold by Elisabeth Elliot in *These Strange Ashes* (San Francisco: Harper and Row, 1975), 132.

Chapter 10: Serious Laughter

1. E.g., Psalms 32; 51; 84; 89.

2. Eugene H. Peterson, *A Long Obedience* (Downers Grove, Ill.: InterVarsity Press, 1980), 96.

3. See, e.g., Numbers 6:25–6; Psalm 2:4; Zephaniah 3:17.

4. C. S. Lewis, *The Last Battle* (San Francisco: HarperCollins, 1994), 46.

5. Flannery O'Connor, *Mystery and Manners* (New York: Straus and Giroux, 1969), 167.

6. G. K. Chesterton, *The Common Man* (New York: Sheed and Ward, 1950), 157–58.

7. Dorothy Thompson, *The Courage to Be Happy* (Cambridge, Mass.: Riverside Press, 1939), 4.

Chapter 11: More Than Words

1. Thomas B. Costain, *The Three Edwards* (Garden City, N.Y.: Doubleday, 1958), 176–80.

2. Samuel Chadwick, quoted by George Verwer, *Come, Live, Die* (Wheaton, Ill.: Tyndale, 1972), 83.

3. James H. Wakelin Jr., "Thresher, Lesson and Challenge," *National Geographic* (June 1964): 104–6.

4. John Bentley, *The Thresher Disaster* (Garden City, N.Y.: Doubleday, 1974), 30.

Chapter 12: Good Things Run Wild

1. Tim Keller, "Preaching Morality in an Amoral Age," *Leadership* (Winter 1996): 112.

2. Albert Einstein, quoted by Laura Schlessinger, *How Could You Do That?* (New York: HarperCollins, 1996), 7.

3. Charles Colson, *A Dangerous Grace* (Dallas: Word, 1994), 61–62.

4. C. S. Lewis, quoted by Rebecca Manley Pippert, *Hope Has Its Reasons* (New York: Harper and Row, 1989), 158.

5. Michel Quoist, *The Christian Response* (Dublin: Gill and Macmillan, 1965), 4.

6. Robert A. Briner, *Squeeze Play* (Grand Rapids, Mich.: Zondervan, 1994), 108.

7. Ruth A. Walton, "The Beggar," *Eternity* (July 1972): 31.